TEST-TAKING POWER

TEST-TAKING POWER

Fred Orr

A Monarch Book
Published by Prentice Hall Press
New York, New York 10023

First published in 1984
George Allen & Unwin Australia Pty Ltd
8 Napier Street, North Sydney NSW, 2060 Australia

Illustrations © 1986 by Peter Meldrum

A Monarch Book
Published by Prentice Hall Press
A Division of Simon & Schuster, Inc.
Gulf + Western Building
One Gulf + Western Plaza
New York, New York 10023

PRENTICE HALL PRESS is a trademark of Simon & Schuster, Inc.

Manufactured in the United States of America

1   2   3   4   5   6   7   8   9   10

Library of Congress Cataloging-in-Publication Data

Orr, Fred.
  Test-taking power.

  "A Monarch book."
  1. Examinations—Study guides.   2. Study, Method of.
I. Title.
LB3060.57.O77   1986   371.2'6   86-2516
ISBN 0-671-61457-6 (pbk.)

Contents

answer questions — Performing in open book examinations —
Performing in laboratory examinations

Panic attacks — Memory blocks — Writer's cramp —
Physical fatigue

External secondary education examinations — The medical
viva examination — Civil service entrance examinations —
Auditions in the performing arts — Time-saving for part-time
students — The job interview — Motor vehicle driver's test

Acknowledgements

Writing a book is singularly hard work, but far from a single effort. I would like to take this opportunity to thank my wife, Rachel, and my three children who unselfishly tolerated my absences and silences while the book was being written. Thanks are also due to Dr Pat Cleary and my colleagues at the Student Counselling and Research Unit at the University of New South Wales for their helpful support and constructive commentary. I would like to extend my thanks and sincere appreciation to my agent, Jill Hickson, for her very sound advice and her helpful understanding during all phases and with all people connected with the project. My thanks are also extended to Carol Serventy for her careful reading of the completed manuscript.

Preface

Examinations, in all of their varied forms, affect just about every one of us during our lives. The formal school years present our first exposure to examinations, but the formal assessment process does not end there. Even after leaving formal education behind, many will confront other types of examinations such as employment interviews (actually an oral examination) and motor vehicle driving tests.

Over the last twelve years, I have seen large numbers of people come to the Counselling Unit of the University of New South Wales with many and varied problems associated with examinations. The concerns brought by the clients range from anxiety reactions about being assessed to muscle cramping during the examinations. Memory blocking, time management and organizational problems are other issues confronting the examination candidates.

As jobs continue to be scarce and the competition keen, the pressure upon students rises. Unless they perform very well, the examination candidates might not get the job they prefer at the end of their course. Thus, preparing thoroughly and performing well in examinations are very important to students today—and the concern is likely to continue.

How can an examination candidate's preparation and performance be improved? For a start, the candidate should read this book. The book presents thirteen concise and practical chapters featuring skills on: how to organize one's study and review; how to relax and control anxiety; how to enhance the basic learning functions, such as memory and concentration; and, finally, how to deal with various types of examinations on examination day.

The book is based upon well-established behavior modification principles which can help you to improve your preparation and performance. But, first you must know how to get started—and the earlier the better. That is the first message of the book—GET STARTED NOW. Readers will very soon discover the second message—KEEP WORKING ON A REGULAR BASIS. Having learned the fundamental truths at the core of this book, you will want to know how these truths can be put into action. Read on.

You will probably benefit by first reading the contents and noting those chapters which have immediate importance and relevance. As will be stated later, becoming more efficient when time is limited is a critical skill for any examination candidate. So, go first to the chapters which address your specific needs. Learn the skills which will enhance your examination success and, as time permits and circumstances warrant, deal with the other chapters and issues at a later time.

A few words about the results of examinations and their effects upon motivation. If you have had mainly successful experiences with examinations so far and you are reading this book to improve still further, well and good. On the other hand, if your examination experiences have been less positive, read and learn from this book and then *actively* apply the principles at every opportunity. Learning new skills, and perhaps, changing old and counter-productive habits, is hard work. Every application of the skills and principles in this book will offer you a valuable learning opportunity. By learning from your experiences, both positive and negative, you will improve your performance.

At this point, I wish you happy reading of the book and good luck with your examinations.

F. E. Orr
Sydney

This book is dedicated to
Matthew, Vanessa and Katharine

TEST-TAKING POWER

1
Getting organized

'How can I get organized for my exams?' That question is asked very frequently by most examination candidates, and the frequency increases as the examination date comes closer. Some students choose a variation on the theme and state, 'Some day I *must* get organized!'

Few people will deny the fact that a well-organized approach to any task is likely to produce a better result. Performing well on your examinations is no exception. This chapter will present several strategies which will help you to organize your studies and yourself for your examinations.

Identifying organizational pitfalls

Take a few minutes and consider the following items. Tick those items which identify common experiences for you, especially in relation to examination preparation and performance.

( ) My days are frequently wasted doing unimportant things.
( ) My work tends to get done in a 'helter-skelter' fashion.
( ) I often have difficulty sorting major concepts from the details.
( ) My examination results would be better if I were able to organize my review better.
( ) I find that I often start tasks, but do not finish them.
( ) I am frequently indecisive about what to do next.
( ) I often find that I am repeating work unnecessarily.

Undoubtedly, there are many more variations on the organizing theme. However, your responses to the checklist will give you some indication about how well you have organized your examination preparation in the past. But let's not dwell on the past, but turn to the future and see how your organizing skills can be improved.

Long-term organizational planning

Your long-term plans might be aimed at a particular career or they might be aimed at a qualification requiring several years of study. While career and life plans are very important, let us focus upon a period of fourteen weeks, a typical academic semester.

Most students do not want to think about the examinations which are lurking at the far end of the semester, a long time away. Indeed, to plan for examinations which come at the end of the year might seem foolhardy, but is this really so? Not at all. Time management experts will readily tell you that the small amount of time spent planning your tasks will pay dividends throughout the work period and at the conclusion of the period. How can the study period preceding the examinations be better organized? Read on!

A fact of life for most examination candidates is that they have too much to do and simply not enough time to do it in. Because of the pressures imposed by other tasks such as reports, assignments and domestic responsibilities, review for examinations usually is put off until just before the examination period. While no one will deny the pressures which bear down upon examination candidates

Semester-at-a-Glance Chart

	Weeks													
	1	2	3	4	5	6	7	8	9	10	11	12	13	14
A				Ass.						Ass.				Exam
B			Rpt.		Tst.		Rpt.					Prj.		Exam
C			Ess.							Ess.				Exam
D							Tst.					Prj.		Exam

Key: Tst = test Ass = assignment Ess = essay
Rpt = report Prj = project

throughout the course of study, it is very important to organize your review *early* and review *regularly*.

'Easily said, but not so easily done!' you might respond. Yes, that's true, but let's consider a method which might help you to get your long-term review organized.

The chart which follows shows the fourteen weeks of the academic semester numbered across the columns, and the subjects listed on the left in the rows. Within the various columns opposite the respective subjects are noted the various assignments, tests and other commitments of the student.

The chart above is fairly typical of the commitments expected of a full-time student. A similar chart can be prepared by examination candidates who are not full-time students by including various work or domestic tasks in the place of some subjects.

There are several important features to note in the chart. One, you can see at a glance where your busy periods are. For example, from the chart it is apparent that weeks four to six and weeks ten to twelve are heavy. With four major study-related events occurring in each of these periods, it will probably be too late to start preparing for various commitments within these periods.

The second feature of the chart is implied in the foregoing comments about 'being too late'. That is, if you want to do a good preparation job for your various tasks, including review for your examinations, then you must give yourself adequate lead-up time. You will note that each of the entries on the chart has a dotted arrow leading up to it. The length of the arrow represents the amount of time needed for preparation.

While discussing lead-up time, you will undoubtedly have noticed that the longest dotted lines lead up to the final examinations in week fourteen. Are you surprised or even shocked to see that the review period for the final examinations starts in week two? If you are, you will not be alone, for most people who have to face an examination in the future simply do not want to think about an event that far ahead.

However, thinking ahead is exactly what you should be doing if you want to maximize your chances of excelling in the examinations. No matter what types of examinations you will be facing at the end of the semester, you will have to know your notes and other study materials if you are to perform well. Reviewing stacks of notes takes time. For most students there will probably not be sufficient time in the final few weeks to carry out these learning tasks well, especially if you are still trying to complete essays and other assignments.

In order to keep your major commitments prominently in mind, make a chart similar to the one presented and record your assignments and any other time-consuming obligations (like a camping weekend). By placing your chart in front of you at your study place, you will be able to see at a glance what your commitments are. With your projects, assignments and examinations clearly in view, you will be reminded to plan ahead and to organize your work and your review with sufficient lead-up time.

To summarize in a few words:

START EARLY
REVIEW REGULARLY

Organizing your days, each day

Early and regular review for your examinations should start by allocating a review period each day before the examinations.

Most people plan their days by trying to remember the tasks and chores which they have to carry out. If your life is fairly complicated, you might have found in the past that your memory has let you down. You've forgotten to buy that anniversary card for a relative; or you've overlooked paying the telephone bill; or you simply forgot to get down to reviewing for an examination early enough. All of these oversights could have dire consequences! Granted, none of us like to forget important things; so how can we ensure that we will remember? One way is to plan your days by writing out a *daily plan*. Childish? Never!

Organizing your days by writing a daily plan is more than just drawing up a list of tasks and chores. There are three important elements in an effective daily plan: (a) a precise description of the item; (b) an allocation of a priority ranking; and (c) an estimate of the time to be spent working on the item. A fourth feature of a successful daily plan is something which you add after the items are completed—a tick (written with gusto!). Let's look at a sample daily plan.

DAILY PLAN

The Jobs	Priority	Time	Done
Math probs p. 103	1	1 hr	
Plan Engl. essay	2	15"	
Read Ch. 5, History	2	1 hr	
Plan Chem. Lab.	1	30"	
Review Unit 14, Comput'g	1	30"	
TV Docmnt'y (Biology)	3	30"	
Call Peter, film Friday	3	10"	

It is important to note the following points about the daily plan:

- The jobs are precisely spelled out.
- Each job has a time length—very important, especially when

telephoning Peter! It might be a good idea to set an egg timer for the stipulated ten minutes.

- The 'Done' column is provided to reinforce the feeling of accomplishment when you have completed a task. Don't dismiss this reinforcement. Examination study can be a grueling task; and a list full of ticks at the end of a day can provide that well-earned feeling of accomplishment. You might even consider patting yourself on the back and saying, 'Well done!' to add to the positive feeling.

- The jobs and the time allotments are precise. It is far better to sit down to a task which is specifically defined for a set amount of time than to approach your studies with the general aim to 'do a bit of studying'. An approach such as this robs you of the feeling that you've completed the task. It's much like the difference between breaking the tape at the finish line of a race and running around the race course but not knowing where the finish line is.

- When preparing your daily plan, take account of the amount of total study time over the semester or term which you think you will need. Your study time will probably vary, depending upon your assignments and the proximity of the examination period.

- Remember, an examination candidate's week has to contain seven days, not just five. Don't forget to prepare a daily plan on the weekends to maximize your effectiveness.

- Please note that studying can be done in short spurts; as short as one or two minutes. While waiting for a bus you could review the basic ideas from your previous day's class notes. Be prepared for these short waiting periods and have review cards or other materials at hand. More will be said about using your time efficiently in the next chapter.

- When preparing your daily plan, look ahead to the next several weeks so that you can devote the necessary lead time to the large tasks. Don't forget to include regular review sessions for the exams at the end of the semester!

Check list to make the daily plan *work*

( ) Establish a regular study routine which includes systematic review for your examinations (more on this in the following section).

( ) Write a daily plan every day.

( ) Set realistic tasks and time goals to maximize your chances of success.

( ) Attempt to accomplish your high priority goals each day.

( ) Add variety to your daily work pattern, and don't neglect physical exercise; you could go for a two-mile walk (or fifteen minute walk) before you tackle your review.

( ) Be certain to maximize the reward value of ticking the items on task completion.

( ) Periodically assess your daily plan, and ask yourself whether you could be organizing your days in a more efficient way.

( ) Say 'NO!' to people who are unnecessarily intruding into your daily plan. Yes, it's a difficult word to say under these conditions, but practicing with tact and diplomacy will perfect your skill.

( ) Plan ahead for your recreational needs and use special leisure events as rewards for high priority work getting done.

( ) Plot on a graph the number of examination review hours spent per week and place the graph in a conspicuous place.

( ) Schedule time for creative thinking and problem solving. . . higher order planning.

( ) Feel good about becoming more organized, and about becoming more prepared for your examinations.

Systematizing your review

Having discussed long and short-term organizational strategies to help you prepare for your examinations, let us turn to several related issues which concern examination candidates.

One issue which they always raise is the matter of how much time should be spent studying each week. The question is a very general one and the difficulty in framing an answer is that every person is unique. What works well for one person may prove to be totally inapplicable to the next. The best way to arrive at a workable solution to the time problem is to do more work than you feel is necessary. If your results are satisfactory, you may then be able to make 'your system' more efficient so that you get more work done in less time. If, however, the time you spent did not reap the desired results, then consult a counselor or a person involved with your course to discuss your whole study approach.

A second concern involves different systems of review for different types of subjects. For example, the review system you would use for a mathematics examination should be quite different from your review approach to an examination in English Literature.

Learning of concepts will apply to most types of examinations. Learning of processes is generally involved in any type of examination where you will be expected to solve problems. Mathematics and physics are just two examples of subjects in which you will have to know how to recognize and then carry out certain types of problem-solving processes. There is no easy answer to preparing for these types of examinations. The essential feature of your review should be many, many working sessions with typical problems. It is to be hoped that, having worked through a large number of sample problems, you will recognize the processes required to solve the problems in the examination and then be able to work through them correctly to reach the right answer.

One further note on reviewing for problem-solving subjects is important. Do not put off the task until the final few days before the examination. Most subjects which involve problem-solving are organized on a plan of increasing complexity. That is, understanding the early work is necessary for working satisfactorily on the later work. So, if you experience difficulties with problems in the early weeks of the course, be sure to get the extra assistance immediately so that you are not at risk later.

While problem-solving subjects require systematic practice, subjects based upon the study of ideas and concepts require a different approach. In subjects like history, geography and literature, your task will be to learn the central ideas and associated details. Your learning will have to be thorough, for when you enter the examination room, the questions will require you to synthesize, associate and then produce a logically derived and concisely written essay. If, perchance, you confront a multiple choice examination, you will still have to know the material, but even more thoroughly, as there is no opportunity to explain your response. You are either right or wrong. More will be said about multiple choice examinations and other types of assessment formats in a later chapter.

In addition to being subject-specific in your approach to examination preparation and review, you would also be well advised to take into account your own strengths and weaknesses. Most people prefer to work on projects which are high in personal interest. However, the examination candidate is often caught in the invidious position of having to apportion review time across a range of subjects, some of which may be very low on the interest dimension. If you find yourself putting off reviewing a particular subject, ask yourself: 'Why?' Generally, the subjects in which you are weakest are going to demand the most review time. Putting them off until another day will just increase the problem.

A further point about systematizing your study concerns *periodic review.* Most examined subjects can be divided into a number of major concepts. It is far preferable to review each major concept as you go through the course. For example, review topic A which was covered in the first two weeks of the course at the end of week two. Review the topic by going through your notes several times. Prior to reviewing topic B in another few weeks, take a few minutes and go through your notes on topic A again. By using this incremental approach systematically throughout the period of study, the material will be well in hand by the end of the course.

One final point about reviewing your notes warrants emphasis. That is, avoid recopying your notes. While reviewing your notes with pen in hand is a good policy, trying to copy what might be sloppy or disorganized notes is a very time-expensive task. And time is usually in short supply! Try experimenting with various notetaking procedures so as to improve the quality of your notes. If you continue to have difficulty with notetaking, see a counselor about the problem.

SUMMARY

In order to become more organized in your examination preparation, start early and review regularly. This chapter has discussed two ways in which you should organize yourself for your examinations—(1) prepare a chart of your week-by-week commitments and (2) write out a daily plan every day to organize your time and plan your priorities.

To help establish a firm and reliable basis for your review, experiment with various review systems. We are all different, and what works for one person is not necessarily going to work for another. When experimenting with various systems, the most workable (the emphasis is upon 'work') approach should take into account several aspects—the total amount of time available for study, your strengths and weaknesses in your subjects, and the types of subjects you are studying (e.g., science or mathematics versus arts and humanities).

To reiterate an important point, regular review of your notes is best done periodically through the semester or term. A good time to sit down and go through your notes is at the completion of a unit of work. By consolidating the concepts at that point, you increase your understanding for later work and you decrease the learning load which would otherwise fall upon you prior to your examinations.

2
Becoming disciplined

How often.....

- Have you sat down at your desk and spent the next two hours shuffling your notes from one side of your desk to the other?
- Have you opened a text to 'do some reading' and found yourself staring blankly at the same page one hour later?
- Have you waited until the night before a report was due to pick up your pen to start writing?
- Have you 'tuned out' in a class because you were not interested in the topic?
- Have you become bogged down when trying to write the first paragraph of a major assignment?
- Have you waited until a week before an examination to begin a systematic review?

The 'how oftens' could go on and on. The list suggests an almost bottomless pit into which examination candidates can fall. Can you recognize the pit? It is the absence of personal discipline.

Unfortunately, many examination candidates, heavily laden with books and stacks of notes, stagger along the pitted road to the examination room. Aside from incurring many psychological bumps and bruises (guilty conscience and dented ego from not getting the work done), the candidates also suffer from decreased performance in the examinations. How often have you heard a classmate or yourself say; 'Had I really worked, I could have done much better'.

This chapter addresses the issue of self discipline. Initially, the topic of procrastination will be dealt with.

Overcoming procrastination

Five steps are presented below to help you get down to work and then progress with your preparation.

Step 1   Get settled!

Preparing for examinations can be—and often is—an anxiety-laden affair. Because of the anxiety and restlessness, many people experience a pronounced difficultly in getting to their desks and becoming settled. They often find that they are simply too jumpy and jittery to get down to work. The first fifteen or thirty minutes can be spent just settling down. As stated before and will be stated again, time is at a premium for most examination candidates. Even fifteen minutes of non-productive time is a luxury which few can afford. How can you get yourself settled more quickly and effectively?

At the risk of sounding like a promoter for hyperactive behavior, may I suggest that prior to sitting down to study, spend just a minute doing some vigorous exercise like running on the spot, doing push-ups, sit-ups, or using a skipping rope. Why? Because the activity can release some of the pent-up steam in your system. As well as getting the restlessness out of your mind and body, the exercise will also stimulate you for productive work. Most people feel good after a spell of exercise, and feeling good and positive are very good feelings to have at the start of a study session.

In addition to exercising prior to studying, you might also try putting on a particular shirt, sweater or even hat—some type of clothing which you find comfortable. The reason for suggesting a particular 'uniform' for your study sessions is that the very act of putting on your study clothes can create the very positive expectation that you are preparing for work. An additional advantage is that any potential distractors, such as friends or family members, can be trained to recognize the uniform as a personalized DO NOT DISTURB sign.

Having exercised briefly and then seated yourself at your study place, make certain that you have all of the materials you need ready at hand. Remember, one of the pitfalls for procrastinating people is jumping up to get this and do that, thus putting off the start of the task. So, carry out an equipment and materials check at the very start. Once you have checked that you have the necessary books, notes, pens, paper and any other materials, *stay seated*. Anything else which pops into your mind should wait until your first break. By the way, drinks and a toilet visit should also be thought about *before* you get seated.

Step 2 Define the task

Many examination candidates approach their review in a much too general way. They will say to themselves; 'I think I'll do a bit of review for the exams tonight'. If by chance an enticing distraction occurs (a friend suggests that they go to a movie), they can then justify to themselves that they have done some studying and therefore can go to the movie.

Defining the task will help to focus your attention upon the end result—performing to your optimum level in the examinations. Additionally, the task definition should focus upon the precise targets for your present study session. As emphasized in the preceding chapter, it is very important to plan your review and be task and time specific. That is, stipulate exactly what you intend to do in each hour or half hour.

When defining your review tasks, pay particular attention to the size of the job and any special aspects, such as laboratory exercises, field trip notes, etc. It is important for your task definition to be as clear and accurate as possible.

Step 3 Divide tasks into manageable parts

One of the most intimidating aspects of examination review is the very size of the task. Looking at what seems to be a mountainous stack of notes and books can create fear (more about this in a later chapter) with resultant escape behavior.

What can you do about the growing size and complexity of the review task? The best way to approach most large and complex jobs is to try to break them down into manageable tasks. Returning to the mountain analogy, one way of moving a mountain is to steadily take away an armful of rocks. Sounds tedious and unpleasant, but it will do the job.

Fortunately, reviewing for your examinations is not likely to take as long or be as tedious. However, the same basic strategy can apply. Look over your notes and pick out the basic concepts and issues dealt with during the semester. For convenience, say that you identify ten major concepts which are examinable. Now, imagine the notes stacked, concept by concept, on your desk. Still looks a bit frightening, doesn't it? But, take the notes on concept one and place them in front of you. Not nearly as bad now, is it? In fact, you can go even further by dividing concept one into relevant subconcepts in order to set your sights upon a realistic study goal for the next review session.

Step 4   *Establish target deadlines*

This step is almost self-explanatory. The final deadline for examination review tasks will be examination day. However, it is helpful to work on shorter deadlines to promote the review effort. For example, establish quarterly and half semester deadlines. In some cases, this will be built-in to your semester if you have half-semester examinations. Another approach would be to establish your deadlines according to the units of work covered or the concepts dealt with in class. The reason for using a deadline system in your review is that it gives you target dates upon which you can pace your work.

Step 5   *Set specific rewards for work done*

Procrastination is for most people a well-established and strong habit. In order to change this habit, you will have to find positive prompters or rewards to reinforce a new kind of behavior—punctuality, reliability, perseverance.

'Enough! Enough!' you might be shouting. Yes, these are powerful behavior patterns and can be a substantial threat to most of us who like to get on with our lives in our own good way, in our own time. However, most examination candidates would not dispute the utility and benefits to be derived from knowing that they can depend on themselves to cover the review material regularly and thoroughly.

What kinds of prompters and rewards can be used to help you develop those positive qualities listed above? The rewards really depend upon what you, as an individual, like. Perhaps eating an orange, taking a brisk walk, phoning a friend (set timer and alarm!) might appeal to you as a sample of rewards which can be used for reinforcing non-procrastinating behavior. However, you might wish to compile your own list of rewards. Think about the things which give you a lot of pleasure and note them on a sheet of paper. It might be helpful to exclude items such as 'getting away from my studies', or 'going on a nine month holiday'. The object of this exercise is to identify a range of reinforcers which you can use in the short term—several times an evening for work accomplished.

How do you make the system work? The answer is implied in the paragraph above, but the issue of reducing procrastination is sufficiently important to warrant reiteration. At every significant stage of your review process, reward yourself for positive progress. For example, if having done some preliminary physical exercise allows you to sit down with a positive attitude about getting into your work, then try rubbing your hands together briskly for a few seconds. The gesture of rubbing your hands together can be pleasurable and it also seems to be associated with the expectation of productivity.

The important principle in making a personal reward system work for you is to have a real set of rewards available and then use them with each forward step. Be careful not to allow the rewards to take pre-eminence over the target task—getting to and through your review.

Practical problems with procrastination

Having discussed the five steps to deal with procrastination, it is necessary to be a realist and ask the question; 'What if the strategy doesn't work?'

If you have tried steps one through to five on several different occasions and still haven't been able to get down into your examination preparation, then you should ask yourself the following questions:

- Am I feeling so fearful about the examinations that any contact with notes and books seems to prevent me from getting to work?
- Am I a perfectionist who must achieve at a 100% level all of the time?
- Does criticism from people close to me (family, friends) interfere regularly with my work?

The first of these issues, fear of examinations, will be dealt with in detail in a later chapter. The other two issues go beyond the scope of this book. However, you should consult a professionally-trained counselor to discuss any residual problems which are preventing you from making significant progress in your examination preparation. Problems will not disappear if you ignore them. Recognize them, and seek assistance in solving them.

In summary, overcoming procrastination can be a major undertaking but, like moving a mountain, can be accomplished with steady work and appropriate rewards. The five step program described above should help you get underway and if you practice regularly, the review process should no longer be seen as an insurmountable mountain but a series of pleasant hills and dales which are a joy to walk through.

Being diligent

For the very diligent and disciplined student, most of this book will be 'old hat'. However, for the vast majority of students who leave their review until late in the year, diligence and discipline may be elusive states about as attainable as the oasis mirage on the desert horizon. Diligence and discipline are very important goals to be pursued but often hard ones to realize.

How can the examination candidate maximize these desirable, yet elusive qualities? Perhaps an R-type acronym might be appropriate: be Rigorous; establish a Routine; and make review a Ritual.

Be rigorous

Becoming rigorous with yourself and your studies might be a difficult exercise, especially if your study habits have been as rigorous and as disciplined as a plate full of boiled spaghetti. However, all is not lost if you have the determination to work diligently and conscientiously through the next x (x = number of weeks until the examination period) weeks. It will take a bit of grit, but deep down within your inner resources, you are bound to find some hidden reserve which can be used. Talk to a close friend or a trusted adviser (a teacher or lecturer?) who has the ability of finding those talent reservoirs. You are confronting a very challenging task which will require a very strong effort over the next few weeks. Every day, indeed, almost every hour, has to count. Arrange a meeting with your outside helper on a regular basis to report on your progress and to get motivated for the next study effort.

If you are planning to motivate yourself by dangling a self-made diploma in front of yourself or by some other devious or legitimate means, it is a good idea to assess your progress daily. Compare the amount of work completed to your goals. Plan a celebration on the far side of your exams but, for the present, get into the review.

Establish a routine

The second R, establishing a routine, may be less difficult. Fortunately we are all, to some extent, creatures of habit and routine. Think back over your early morning activities. You probably brushed your teeth at the same point in your order of events today as you did yesterday, and you will probably do so tomorrow. Just as you dress, eat and leave your house or room in a routine order on most days, you can apply the same behavioral pattern to your review. That means setting a time and place for your exam review and being there and ready to go at the appointed time. Establishing a routine can make your review task considerably easier, for you are not faced with the decision; 'Should I get to work now, or do X, Y or Z?' The answer has already been decided for you at the start of the preparation period.

During the initial days, when you might experience some difficulty adhering to your newly-established routine, set an alarm or ask a friend to remind you that 'it is now seven o'clock.' The time signal should activate your study behavior or at least get you moving to your desk. After a few days, you will find it easier and easier to get down to the books and notes at the set time.

Make review a ritual

The final R of this 3R acronym stands for making review a ritual.

Part of the ritual will be getting to your place of study at the appointed time. Once there, you might think of your study efforts as somewhat akin to carrying out a religious ritual. As noted elsewhere in this book, a certain amount of prayer might not go astray, especially for some last minute reviewers. But, for the more conscientious student, think about applying various activities to your study effort. For example, after having been at your desk or table for an hour, you might consider a change, such as standing and reciting some of the material you have been reviewing. Should you be musically talented, why not see if you can hum or sing any relevant information which you have been studying. Silly? Yes, perhaps; but anything you can do to humor yourself along is not wasted effort. Standing, kneeling, reciting, singing (and praying) can function to keep your body and mind alert and receptive. Devise your own rituals which will keep you actively progressing through your notes. There is always a place for imaginative approaches to the most mundane tasks.

With all of the standing, kneeling and singing which was suggested (with a bit of tongue-in-cheek) above, you will find that not only will your mind need an occasional break but your body might be itching for a change as well. Even though you will be sitting comfortably while studying, your body and mind will still fatigue. We all vary in the amount of work which we can tolerate before our efficiency goes plummeting downhill. From your past study efforts, you will probably have some idea about how long you can last before a break is absolutely necessary.

While study breaks are necessary, it is very important that they are just breaks and not terminations. Once again, use a handy alarm or an egg timer and set it for the length of your break. A timer can be especially important if you have decided to ring a friend during your break to discuss your progress.

Apart from timing your breaks, consider trying different types of activities. For example, why not try walking briskly around the block during one of your breaks. On another occasion, try doing some body stretching exercises. On another, you might plan a special treat of watching an important show on television. Beware! The TV set can quickly lull you into a state of mesmerism and sap your powers of discipline and determination. If you are weak-willed with the TV, try standing and not sitting for the show you want to watch. It is strange how it takes so much energy to get up and out of a chair in which you have been sitting for a TV show.

In addition to hourly or so breaks during your day and evening study, you might find it necessary to break away from the home front occasionally. Studying for long periods in the same place can cause some restless feelings in some people. Moving your study place to the library or to another location is not out of the question. However, you might find a strong temptation to go to a friend's place. If the friend is a serious student and you can depend upon your powers of discipline to prevent long conversation from interrupting your progress, then the occasional joint study-session might be beneficial.

SUMMARY

Overcoming procrastination and becoming more diligent can be two of the most challenging problems facing examination candidates. With respect to the former challenge, try the following:

- Get settled earlier and stay seated until a planned break
- Define your study tasks
- Break up large review jobs into more manageable tasks
- Establish deadlines for your review of each subject
- Use rewards to reinforce progress and positive change

Becoming more diligent in review can be enhanced by using a 3R acronym:

- Become rigorous in your studying and review—be firm!
- Establish a review routine and keep to it
- Use rituals in your review to enhance your learning

3
Using your time efficiently

An examination candidate can be aptly described as a person who has too much to do and not enough time to do it. When you consider the demands upon your time, not only from the academic sector of your life, but as well from home, relationships, leisure, and perhaps even a job, it is easy to see that time is at a premium.

This chapter addresses the issue of time. Initially, you will be asked to reflect upon your typical days in order to identify habitually wasted time. Having identified areas of wasted time, some suggestions will be offered on time conservation so that you can invest it in your examination preparation. The chapter will conclude with sections on the use of electronic learning aids and the plight of the part-time student.

Identifying wasted time

Time for an examination candidate is critical, perhaps even more so as the examination date draws near. During this period, time can be a source of anxiety. To some extent, this feeling is attributable to the fact that time is totally inelastic, non-producible and un-repeatable. No matter how much you want an extra day or so to prepare for the examination, there is absolutely no way that the time can be elongated (outside of convincing the examiners that the date should be changed).

Instead of hoping and praying for a delay of the examination, it would be far preferable to identify areas in your daily lifestyle which are typically wasting valuable time and then try to use these periods more productively.

Time-wasters

In order to use time better in the future it is worthwhile identifying how and where you have mismanaged your time in the past. Take a few minutes at the end of each day over the next week and complete the following notes.

> Time-wasters
> Date ___/___/___
> Time-wasting event:
> > When?
> > Where?
> > With whom?
> > Why?
> > Amount of time wasted: _____

Complete these notes for each time-wasting event during the day. Try to be critically analytical in your thinking. For example, ask yourself: 'Did that telephone call of twenty-five minutes really need to take twenty-five minutes?'

Having collected your time-wasting data over a week, sit down and review the information. Do you see any general trends or common events which seem to be frequently taking a considerable amount of your time? List the five most frequent and bothersome wasters of your time.

Having listed your habitual time-wasters, you may be interested to learn what other examination candidates have nominated. High on the list is television. Does that surprise you? Probably not. Following closely behind are: waiting time, telephone calls, travel time, meetings, drop-in visitors and a time-wasting grab bag of items listed under the heading 'inability to say "NO!" finish the list. Let's consider each of these categories from a time-saving perspective.

Time-saving strategies

Television

- Read the program guide and decide which shows warrant watching.
- Realize that turning the TV on requires little energy, but turning it off can be a challenge.
- Set an egg timer or alarm to go off at the end of programs to be viewed.
- If you want to watch only the news, stay standing—do not sit down.
- Place the TV in a high cupboard or position it behind a large piece of furniture. The less conspicuous it is and the more difficult it is to get to, the less you may be tempted to turn it on.
- The definitive solution for the poor self-disciplinarians—sell the set or give it away!

Waiting time

- Always carry a book or some handy notes with you so that while waiting for the bus, train or a friend, you can use the time for review.
- Plan ahead, and anticipate waits. Use the time before a class starts, or before an appointment or a meeting to prepare for the event.
- If you have a doctor's appointment and you have found in the past that the waiting room is generally full on your arrival, telephone ahead and ask what delay is anticipated. Try making an appointment for the first time-slot in another consultation session.
- Waiting in line for a cup of coffee or to be attended to at the

bank can be useful time if you carry some pocket-sized review cards.

Telephone calls

Calls to others:
- Plan for a telephone period daily and do them in bulk.
- Plan each call. What are your objectives? How long should the call take?
- Be fully prepared to say; 'I've got to go now,' to the other party to terminate the call.
- Use the egg timer or an alarm when ringing a person you know is very talkative. Tell them at the start of the conversation that you only have a short time to speak and get on with the matter you rang them for.

Calls from others:
- If you do not want to be disturbed, take the telephone receiver off the hook.
- Do not hesitate to tell the other party that you are busy and that you will ring back when you are free.
- For frequent callers, tell them when you would prefer to be rung—ideally during your telephone period.
- If possible, have your calls screened and messages taken so that you are not unnecessarily disturbed.

Travel

- Time on public transport or in your car be used productively.
- On crowded buses and trains, carry palm-sized cards with new terms, formulae and other memory chores so that your sitting or standing time is learning time.
- In your car, use a tape recorder to play back important lectures or your own self-recorded notes.
- When in heavy city traffic, use the pauses when in traffic jams or at red lights to make necessary notes on a pad.
- Think about the weather, available space and the amount of time which you generally experience in your daily travels and adapt your notes and review practice to these conditions.

Drop-in visitors

- Keep your door closed if you do not want to be disturbed.

- For persistent intruders, place a firmly worded note on your door.
- If possible, arrange for someone to intercept visitors and take messages for you.
- Go to others before they come to you. It is easier to terminate conversations when you are at their place.
- If they come to you, stand in the doorway of your room and discuss the matter there.
- If they do get into your room, do not sit down and do not offer them a seat if you want the meeting to be brief. Standing conversations tend to be far shorter that those carried on while sitting.
- Practice terminating phrases, such as; 'Well, then, it seems that . . .' to give notice to the other party that you want to draw the conversation to a close.

Inability to say 'NO!'

- Anticipate events where you are likely to be asked to take on responsibilities which you do not want to accept.
- Practice saying 'NO!' to the bathroom mirror. Exaggerate the word, say it emphatically. With practice in private, it's much easier to say it in public.
- Saying 'NO!' assertively (a positive and constructive communication) can be a complex and delicate task. If you are not successful after trying several times, consult a professionally trained counselor to discuss the matter.

Using electronic learning aids

Using electronic aids, such as a tape recorder to study past lectures while you are in a car has already been suggested earlier in this chapter. Tape recorders have been the focus of interest by students for many years. There seems to be a lingering myth that, by recording your class notes on to tape and then playing it repeatedly throughout the night with the speaker under your pillow, you will learn the material effortlessly. This myth is totally unfounded. The only result of using a tape playback of class notes while you are sleeping is likely to be broken sleep which will reduce your efficiency the next day.

In addition to playing back tapes while traveling in a car, a recorder can also be used at any time when your mind is not being actively absorbed by other matters.

A mature-age student who had a part-time catering business found that she could use much of the food preparation time as learning time. She prepared tapes by recording the vocabulary terms, conjugations and declensions (she was a language student!) with response time between each item. While her hands were busy cooking, her mind could be reviewing vital information for her classes and examinations.

With the advent of video tape recorders in homes and educational institutions, the same practice as noted above is theoretically possible using video feedback. There seems little usefulness in using video over audio tape playback unless the subject matter which you are studying is visual in content. For example, a fine arts student might find that taping slides of famous buildings, paintings, or sculptures might be a useful way of reviewing for the relevant examinations. In similar fashion, a drama student could review plays, especially focusing upon the technical aspects of the taped productions.

There seems little doubt that the personal computer is likely to have the most significant impact of all electronic instruments upon educational systems, student learning practices and even examination preparation. To mention a particularly immediate application of the personal computer, this book was written using a computer with word processing software.

Personal computers are now becoming a very common sight in media advertisements and in homes. It can be a bit frightening to think that in the future you may have to learn about computers, if only to keep pace with the new generation of 'computerized' school students. Confronting our own fears can require courage, but the benefits will certainly be worthwhile. To offset the fears, it should be mentioned that the computer can save time and help the examination candidate to become more efficient.

A word of warning seems appropriate at this point. Computers can be almost addictive in their influence, especially with the newly-converted. If you think that putting your class notes into a computer and retrieving all facts, figures and concepts which relate to a particular topic is going to be your salvation in preparing for your examinations, don't get too excited. The computer can only process what you have placed into it and then it can only act upon this information by using special programs. And, generating these programs can be a very involved task. If computer science is your field of study, then perhaps you can justify the time as practical experience. If you have no knowledge about programing, then you are well advised to stick to your more orthodox study routine.

The time constraints on part-time study

Part-time study raises some particularly difficult challenges for the examination candidate. Being a full-time worker and part-time student can be a hectic existence: work all day and study most nights. Weekends become absorbed in catching up on past reading and report preparation. There seems to be little or no time for anything else. Such a life could suit an academic recluse, but most people look for more in life than just work and study.

In order to meet your needs for pursuing your relationships and your leisure, not to mention sleeping and eating, you will have to become a very time-conscious person. Virtually every minute of the day will have to be used effectively and efficiently in order to fit in all of the activities which you want to pursue.

Think creatively about opportunities for opening up some study time where there previously wasn't time. For example, approach your employer and ask if you can have time in lieu of work for up to four or five hours a week (more if you can argue the case). The request will be perfectly appropriate if your course of study relates directly to the type of work which you are doing. Some firms and institutions have study leave built into their working conditions for various positions.

If your work is at home with child care and domestic duties, there could be a similar opportunity. Discuss with your partner or a friend the possibility of taking an afternoon off from the domestic scene to pursue your studies. If that is not possible, your studies will simply have to fit into your daily routine. Try the tape playback method at the sink or while house cleaning. Make maximum use of the time when the children are sleeping. After putting your feet up for a brief rest, put your mind into your studies. By carefully looking over your typical days, you can probably find small bits of time here and there which could be used more efficiently.

SUMMARY

Examination candidates face at least a two-fold challenge—reviewing the material *and* finding the time for the review. Efficient time management starts with identifying time-wasting activities or inactivities. Critically evaluate your time commitments to the following:

- Television watching
- Idle waiting time
- Unnecessarily long telephone calls
- Commuting time
- Drop-in visitors
- Time wasted because you could not say 'NO!'

The recent advent of the electronic age has put audio tape recorders, video recorders and home computers within reach and use of many examination candidates. In addition to the uses suggested in this chapter, think about other possible uses of these devices which could help you to become more efficient in your preparation for examinations.

4
Learning how to relax

One of the most common problems involving examinations is
severe anxiety or nervousness. In addition to the fact that the level
of outcome of the examinations can have quite drastic effects upon
the future of the candidate, the very process of just preparing for
them can be a stressful experience.

This chapter will focus upon three issues relating to examination
anxiety. One, learning over several months how to relax, both
mentally and physically; two, modifying fear reactions to examinations; and three, learning how to relax quickly while in the examination room.

Learning how to relax

Before dealing with the techniques of relaxation, it is worthwhile to consider a checklist of signs and symptoms associated with stress.
When thinking about or doing an examination, does:

- Your heart thump with exaggerated beats at an accelerated rate?
- Your breathing rate increase and become shallow?
- Your body sweat (palms, underarms and face)?
- Your mind become agitated?
- Your stomach feel queasy?

The above list is not exhaustive, but most examination candidates will be able to identify with some, if not all of the above conditions.

If your heart is thumping, your breathing rate is racing, your hands are quivering and wet, and your whole body is shuffling and shifting in your seat, performing in an examination can be much more difficult than it need be.

How do you get control of these problems? One way is to train your mind and body to relax on command.

Relaxation training

It is interesting to note that what we are really aiming at in relaxation training is the power to control effectively what our minds are doing. The human mind is a very active organ and, in most people, the activity of this organ is to some extent autonomous. That is, the mind is like a team of stage coach horses which is racing out of control while the driver is gripping the seat. In order to gain control, the driver has to work hard at tugging and pulling in the reins to reduce the speed and to redirect the team.

The same condition exists for most people entering a training course in relaxation. Because our minds have been subjected to years and years of stimulation, arousal and provocation, with no time being spent on learning how to quiet the mind, it will be hard but enjoyable work acquiring the skill of relaxation. It is important to emphasize that learning how to relax is a long-term project. That is, months of practice will be necessary to achieve the full effect. Don't be put off by the word 'practice' because it is a most pleasant and enjoyable experience. But it will take time.

The following steps will be a helpful guide to learning the skill.

Practice every day

Place relaxation practice on your daily plan and give it a high priority rating. The more you practice, the better you will be able to relax. Even though learning how to relax might sound simple, it's not. You'll have to work at it regularly and conscientiously to perfect the skill.

'How much should I practice each day?' At the start of your training, several short (three-five minutes) sessions will be helpful. At this stage, longer sessions are likely to give you practice in worrying or day dreaming. As you progressively become more skilled in controlling the activity of your mind, increase the length of the sessions. Ultimately, try to practice for about thirty minutes each day, in two 15-minute sessions.

One word of warning: On very busy days, you may be tempted to put off your practice sessions altogether. These are the days when it is most important to relax. So, stick to your routine and turn your mind off to the pressures of the day and on to the relaxation technique. In addition to giving you valuable practice and a well-needed rest, the time spent relaxing is also forming a firm habit of personal discipline—being able to get to and through the important tasks of each day.

Expect to relax

It is important that you develop a positive expectation that you will relax. There is little use in shouting to yourself, 'RELAX, dammit, RELAX!!' You might try instead saying calmly and decisively; 'I am going to relax now'. Relaxation is a passive process which must be practiced. Trying too hard will only complicate the process. Just sit back and let it happen.

Find a quiet spot

You can relax just about anywhere, assuming you can remain undisturbed for a few minutes. If you are at home or in an office, take the telephone off the hook. If others might call in on you, place a 'Do not Disturb' sign on your door. Better yet, tell them you are practicing your relaxation skills before you start. If quiet spots are difficult to find during your days, you can still get on with the job.

Many people have found practicing on commuter buses and trains perfectly satisfactory. Others practice in their cars or stretched out on a sunny or shady spot in a park. The important point is to make certain that you fit the practice into your daily schedule. If you can practice at the same time and place every day, so much the better. Before long, you will find yourself positively anticipating the relaxation period every day.

Make yourself comfortable

As implied in the previous step, you really don't need special conditions in which to practice relaxation. You can sit on a chair, lie on a bed (set an alarm in case you fall asleep, as beds carry the further expectation of going to sleep), or stretch out in a comfortable spot outside. One commuting student even practiced while standing up on crowded trains, although the response tended not to be as deep as he was able to experience at home. At the beginning of your practice session, loosen any tight clothing, unfasten tight shoelaces and remove glasses if they are heavy. Maximize your comfort.

Focus on your breathing

To start, close your eyes and focus your attention upon your breathing. Listen to the soft whistling sound as the air flows in and flows out. Be sure that you are 'belly breathing'. That is, your belly should be moving in and out as you breathe.

After about a minute or two of concentrating on your breathing, start counting sequentially from one to ten on your inhalations and saying to yourself, 'RELAX' as you exhale. For example, on the first inhalation, say 'ONE' and see the number one in your mind. On exhalation, say 'RELAX' and see the word RE—L-A-X-X-X . . . in your mind. Continue the counting process until you feel quiet and your mind is focused and undisturbed by fleeting thoughts.

The counting process is actually a convenient way to prevent extraneous thoughts and ideas from entering your mind and disturbing you. If your mind is actively occupied with sights and sounds of the number sequence followed by the word, 'RELAX', then it will be difficult for other thoughts to distract you. Ultimately, just saying the word, 'RELAX' will evoke the relaxation response in you, but for the present it will be necessary to go beyond this level.

Focus your attention

Focusing your attention might sound easy, but it can be quite difficult, especially for the person with a very active mind. The counting series described in the previous step is a start, but you will want to go further to experience the deepest possible effects of relaxation. Try one or more of the following scenes. Make the scene as real as possible, experiencing as many of the sensual aspects as you can.

Walk through an English garden

I am standing on a small hill overlooking a garden below on a warm and sunny day in early summer. I can feel the sun's warmth on my forehead and cheeks. On the level below, there is a lovely garden bathed in deep, luxurious green and punctuated by numerous flower beds filled with summer flowers. The garden is inviting and I walk over to the marble steps which lead down to the garden.

Starting at the top step, I step down to the next and with each successive step, I can feel myself becoming more and more relaxed. Stepping now down to 18. . .17, feeling the smooth, cool marble under my bare feet. .16. . .15. . .(counting slowly as I exhale) . .14. . .(feeling more and more relaxed) . .13. . .12 . . .11. . .10. .(down and down). . 9. . . 8. .(deeper and deeper). . 7. . . 6. . . 5. . .(very deep now). . 4. . . 3. . . 2. . . and 1. . .

Down at the bottom of the steps, I can feel the warm, soft grass under my feet, and smell the sweet fragrance of the summer flowers hanging heavily in the air. I walk over to a garden statue of a Grecian goddess and touch the smooth surface of the stone. Very smooth, with soft flowing lines. It seems that the sun's rays penetrate and meet somewhere inside the smoky white stone, which is firm to the touch, but soft to the eyes.

Further along in the garden, I come to one of the numerous flower beds with flowers of every color and hue. The fragrance is very sweet and strong. I can smell the perfume as I feel the occasional soft puffs of warm air on the left side of my face.

I approach a large fountain which is spraying fine jets of water into the air. A mist of vapor is picked up by the breeze and I can now feel the fine droplets landing on my face—very cooling, while my face feels quite warm from the sun. The sun's rays create a vivid rainbow in the mist with intense colors of red . . . orange . . . yellow . . . green . . . blue . . . and violet.

Further along in the garden, I come to a large lake with two swans, one black and one white, drifting so peacefully and effortlessly in unison through the water. They glide through lily pads with white, pink and mauve colored flowers. So quiet, tranquil and relaxing. Very, very relaxing.

I sit down on the bank of the lake and then lie back on the soft, warm grass. So comfortable and quiet. I can feel the warm sun basking down and warming my entire body. So relaxed, very relaxed. As I lie there, I am quite alone and free from problems and concerns. Just me, warm and relaxed, alone and quiet by the lake. Very quiet, very tranquil and very calm. . .

At this point you would progress to the next step in the procedure. However, an alternate scene will be presented for those who suffer from hay fever or pollen allergies or for those who simply do not like gardens, lakes, or swans.

South Pacific Island beach

I have gone on a holiday to a remote South Pacific island where all my needs are catered to. Today, I have walked to a distant beach, far removed from any habitation. I am standing at the back of the beach in the shade of some palm trees. I can hear the chirping of some birds overhead and I can hear the rustling of the palm fronds as they move in the gentle wind. Looking out across the golden-white sands of the beach, I can see the blue-green water of the ocean. Glancing further out to sea, the water becomes a rich, intense blue and then terminates in the arc of the horizon. Overhead, one large, puffy white cloud drifts lazily across the sky.

As the day is warm, I decide to go down to the water and step out from the shade of the palm trees. As my foot first makes contact with the sand, I am immediately aware of the lovely warmth. I can feel the warmth radiating up through the soles of my feet into my legs, . . . my abdomen, . . . my chest, . . . arms, . . . neck, . . . and head. So warm, so pleasant. As I walk, almost in slow motion down to the water, I can feel the powdery, soft sand slowly giving way under my feet. The sand is very soft and very fine.

I come to the smooth, cool sand, left damp by the receding tide. The sand is firm but receptive to my feet which leave their mark as I walk. I now walk to the water's edge and then into the water to calf-depth. The water is cool and very refreshing. I look down into the crystalline clear water and I can see on the bottom several fragments of broken shell, a large star fish with purple and blue encrustations on its upper surface. I can see two small crabs scurrying away from me and a small school of silvery fish darting hither and thither. The water is so clean and clear that I scoop up several handfuls and splash it over my body. Very cool and refreshing.

I now walk back up on to the dry sand and stretch out on my beach towel, face upwards. I can feel the penetrating warmth of the sand working its way up into my back. I can feel droplets of water slowly running off the upper surface of my body. The sun warms and dries my body. So warm. . . So pleasant. . .

Lying on the beach, I can only hear the gentle lapping of the waves upon the sand. Occasionally, a sea gull calls as it flies overhead, but apart from these sounds, it is blissfully quiet. So quiet, so calm, . . . so relaxing. . .

Once again, at this point you would progress to the next step of the series. However, it is important to present still another way of concentrating attention especially for those who experience difficulty in forming strong visual images.

The script which follows is a progressive muscle relaxation series. All you are asked to do is to focus upon the muscles mentioned and allow them to release as much tension as possible. It might be helpful to allow the muscle to become loose, flabby, warm or even heavy—any state which you feel is associated with relaxation. Read through the script several times and, when you have put it into practice, pause for about fifteen seconds at each muscle group to allow the muscles to relax.

Progressive muscle relaxation

Focus upon your forehead muscles, just above your eyebrows. Feel them become loose, . . . warm. . . heavy. . . and relaxed. Now down to your eyebrows, . . . very relaxed. Your cheeks and mouth muscles, . . . very loose, . . . very relaxed. Your jaw muscles, . . . nice and loose, letting your lower jaw drop open as it wishes. Now your neck muscles, front and back; letting them become warm, . . . loose, . . . and very relaxed. Not let your shoulders drop as much as they want. . . Notice how good it feels to let that tension go.

Now relax your arms, both of them together. Feel the tension flowing in waves down your arms and out through your fingers. Your arms feel more loose and relaxed with each breath out.

Now your back muscles. Feel them sinking down. . . and down into the chair (bed, grass). . . Just further and further down, . . .down. . .down. . . More and more relaxed. . . Now focus upon your chest muscles. Feel them become more loose and relaxed with each breath out. That's it, very relaxed. And now, your abdominal muscles. Letting the tension go, more and more with each breath out. Very relaxed, . . .warm and relaxed. And finally, your legs. Just let the tension flow down and away, leaving your legs very loose, . . .very relaxed. That's it, very relaxed.

And now, the entire body. Letting the muscle tension go. Feeling very relaxed. Very, . . .very re-lax-x—x—ed. Quiet, . . .calm. . . and . . .re-lax-x—x—ed.

If you are still with me, I should add just one more attention-focusing technique, so that you have a range to select from. One of the major reasons why rigid and inflexible relaxation programs fail is that the user becomes bored. The more variety you can put into your relaxation practice, the greater your motivation to continue practicing is likely to be.

Walking down to your relaxation room

Imagine yourself at the top of a lovely curving staircase. You can see the carpet flowing down and around to the left. You can feel the deep pile of the soft carpet under your bare feet. Your hand is resting upon a smooth wooden bannister. As you descend the stairs, one at a time, you will find yourself feeling more and more relaxed with each step down.

Starting at the top, the twentieth step, you step down to 19. . .now down to 18. . .letting your hand slide down the bannister as you go. . .17 . . .more relaxed with each step down. . .16. . .15. . .14. . . 13. . .feeling the soft carpet under your feet. . .12. . .11. . . 10. . .relaxed, more and more relaxed. . .9. . .8. . .7. . .more relaxed with each breath out. . . 6. . .5. . .4. . .very relaxed now, very relaxed. . . .3. . .2. . . and now, down to 1 . . .very, very relaxed.

Across the landing at the bottom of the stairs you see a large, very thick door which leads into your private room. You walk over to the door and take hold of the door handle and swing it open gently. The door swings smoothly on its hinges and you walk into the room, pulling the door shut behind you. As you shut the door, you leave all of your problems, worries, cares and concerns outside. Inside your private room, you are free from these concerns.

You look about you and notice the lighting in the room. It is your own room and decorated to your own liking. Now you take note of the colors on the walls and furnishings. And now you survey the range of furniture. Finally, you note the carpet or floor coverings.

You now walk over to the most comfortable chair or couch and stretch out, sinking down into the cushions. Almost feeling yourself moving down, . . .down, . . .down into the cushions. The room is so quiet and so relaxing. . .very relaxing. No cares, problems, worries or concerns. Just you. Very peaceful. Very quiet and so. . .so. . .relaxed.

Having dealt with a series of focusing techniques, we are now ready to move on. At this point, it might help if you did some running on the spot to get yourself back into an alert and receptive state. If you were reading the focusing passages to attain a state of relaxation, then delete the running and enjoy your relaxed state.

Positive self-suggestions

The use of positive self-suggestions is a very important part of preparing for examinations. Positive thinking will be discussed more fully in a later chapter; but, the use of positive suggestion will be dealt with here as an adjunct to relaxation training.

When you are relaxed, you will note that your body has slowed down. Your heart rate will be slower, your breathing rate will be slower; in fact most of your bodily functions will be pleasantly slow and easy. Even your mind will be less active, although still aware of what is happening. When your mind is relatively quiet and calm, you can present constructive messages to yourself. While the exact mechanism is unclear, these messages are received and registered by the mind and they can act positively to affect your examination preparation and performance.

It is very important to say, here and now, that using positive self-messages in the absence of any real work and study for your exams will result in a comfortable failure. That is, the practice of relaxing yourself and feeding yourself unrealistically positive messages is not going to produce a magical pass. The procedure is best used to enhance your examination preparation. There is simply *no* substitute for early and regular review for examinations.

Some of the suggestions which you may wish to try are listed below:

- I can relax.
- I can control my mind.
- I can concentrate on my studies.
- I can perform to the best of my ability.

You will note that the suggestions are all 'I can' type statements. They are fairly general in their scope, and are concisely stated. It would be a waste of your time to feed in patently unrealistic messages.

Come back slowly

In order to come out of your relaxed state, count slowly from one to five, feeling yourself becoming more alert with each number. At five, slowly open your eyes and then stretch your arms and legs. Do not get straight up on to your feet, as you might become light-headed.

Note how you feel

Before doing anything else, notice how relaxed you feel. You might feel a sensation of heaviness in your limbs, or perhaps a feeling of dryness in your mouth. Your body might feel lethargic and reluctant to move. Take a minute or so and just enjoy that relaxed and comfortable feeling.

Plan your next relaxation session

While the positive effects of your present relaxation experience are still with you, take time to plan when you will next practice relaxing. Remember, practice is absolutely essential and an organized approach is necessary to learn the skill. After a few weeks of practice, you will probably find that the effects of the relaxation experience are so positive that you are actually looking forward to your next practice session.

It is important to mention that you should be planning to practice on average twice a day for about fifteen minutes each time over a three to four month period to make relaxation a part of your daily routine and a permanent skill. After you have fully learned how to relax, you could go for prolonged periods without relaxing (not that this is recommended) and return to the practice sessions with little or no difficulty. Learning how to relax is much like learning any other skill, such as riding a bicycle or typing. Once learned, the skills are never forgotten. They can be reactivated with little effort at a later time. So, a conscientious three to four month learning period can be seen justifiably as a life-time investment.

Draw up a daily practice chart

As a reminder to carry out your relaxation practice, draw up a chart on which you can record the number of relaxation practice sessions carried out each day. Place the chart on your mirror or dresser top, somewhere you are likely to look at the beginning and end of each day. In addition to recording simply the number of practice sessions per day, you might also want to record the depth of relaxation you attained, perhaps on a scale of five units—one for shallow, down to five for a very deep response. At a glance, then, you can see how your practice is progressing.

Relaxation training is a very positive and pleasant skill to learn just for the sake of dealing with daily stress. However, the skill of controlling and relaxing your mind will have particular benefits before and during examination time. By controlling your mind, you will be able to prevent day-dreaming and faulty concentration. You will also be able to feel more rested and relaxed for your study sessions.

While relaxation training is recommended for just about everyone, it will be particularly important for those candidates who are troubled by excessive anxiety or extreme nervousness before and during their examinations. The relaxation skills described in the preceding part of this chapter are necessary for the use of the anxiety reduction technique described in the next section.

Dealing with fear of examinations

Our bodies can respond quite strongly to scenes we imagine. The ability to respond so strongly can be used to *reduce* the fear associated with examinations. By practicing relaxation training, you can develop a sufficiently strong relaxation response which will then counteract the fear symptoms associated with examinations. This can be done by systematic desensitization, a process which has been extensively studied by psychologists and found to be very effective. In fact, scientific studies have shown that examination candidates who were well-prepared, but very anxious during examinations, experienced up to a thirty per cent increase in their examination marks following a program of systematic desensitization. The emphasis in the last sentence should be placed upon 'well-prepared,' as systematic desensitization will not be able to put the concepts and other critical ideas into your brain. You must do that for yourself.

Have a friend read the following description to you while you sit comfortably with your eyes closed. Try to place yourself in the scene being described.

> You have just arrived outside the examination room and you can see other students flicking through their notes and chatting nervously with each other. You can feel the brittle tension in the air. A classmate dashes up and blurts; 'Did you read the Hopkins chapter on the reading list!?' Your mind immediately sprints into high gear; 'Have I overlooked that reading? What if there are questions on it in the exam? Whose notes can I borrow to have a quick overview?'
>
> Just as you are looking over the crowd, the doors of the examination room are opened and the students start filing in. You enter the room still thinking about that Hopkins chapter and the possibility of a related examination question. You take a seat as a supervisor announces; 'Do not open your examination booklets until instructed to do so!'
>
> You arrange your pens on the desk top and read the grafitti carvings on its wooden surface. You look up nervously and see the supervisors canvassing the room with their stern eyes. Not a smile in sight. The chief supervisor then announces; 'You have three hours to complete this examination. Open your examination booklets and begin.'

Having imagined yourself in the examination room, take note of your heart and breathing rates. If you were able to make the imagery quite real, you might find that your heart rate is accelerated and that you are breathing more rapidly as well.

Using systematic desensitization

As suggested above, systematic desensitization (SD, for short) will help you to reduce the anxiety experienced in examinations. The process is somewhat similar to overcoming the nervousness which a novice swimmer might experience at the thought or act of going into deep water.

The swimmer could construct several stages which lead ultimately to going into the deep water. For example, simply walking along the beach next to the water should present little difficulty. The next step might be walking in calf-deep water, followed by thigh-deep, waist-deep, chest-deep and then floating. While at each step, the novice swimmer would pause until there was no fear or nervousness at being at that particular depth. Then and only then would the swimmer advance to the next step. Of course, the swimmer would be very well-advised to practice assiduously the various swimming strokes so that there would be no danger of drowning once deep water was reached.

The very same process can be carried out for examination anxiety, but in this particular case, it is recommended that you approach the task using vivid imagery. The steps could be constructed along a time dimension instead of space, as was the case in the example above.

Think back to your previous examinations. When did you first notice that you were becoming nervous? At the door of the examination room? The night before? Two weeks before? Or even on day one of the year?

For most examination candidates, thinking about day one of the course would create very little examination fear. We want a very low anxiety level to start, so why not choose day one as the first step of the hierarchy (a term which means a graded series—in this case a series of chronological steps with increasing anxiety as the examination day approaches).

For each step, write a brief description which is as close as possible to your own situation. You might write the notes on small cards, one note per card. When all of the cards have been made, you can then use them one at a time to bring to mind imagery relevant to each step. This is done while you are comfortably relaxed, with the cards lying by your hand or on your chest. You simply relax thoroughly and then read the first scene and imagine it in as much detail as possible. When you are able to imagine the scene and respond with complete relaxation, then you take the next card, read it and then imagine the setting. In like fashion, you move up the hierarchy until you are able to imagine the scene which originally prompted the highest anxiety response with complete, or almost complete, relaxation.

Let's consider a few examples.

Card 1

Day one of the course, and everyone is comparing timetables and talking about the subjects they are taking. Someone mentions how difficult the examinations are in this course. I am standing outside the room where my examinations will be held in four months. I can see the empty desks in the room and the blackboard at the front of the room. There is an electric clock on the far wall which will time the examination.

Card 2

One month before the examinations. I'm sitting at my desk in my room looking at the list of outstanding assignments and thinking about my review for the examinations. Four weeks to go and still so much to do!

You will notice that in the first two cards a considerable time span has elapsed, from day one of the course to one month before the examinations. It is important for you to construct your own hierarchy to fit your own circumstances. Perhaps you need another step or two to bridge what might be too great a gap. Examination fear usually increases as the date of the examinations approaches. Thus, you might need quite a few cards to represent the final week before the examinations.

It is worthwhile to note as well that two different locations were chosen for the first two cards, one in front of a classroom and the second at the student's desk. Many people who experience examination anxiety report that the fear is strongest at certain times (generally, in the days and weeks just prior to the examinations), in certain places (classrooms, laboratories, or other places associated with assessments), and with certain people (teaching staff, some classmates—especially those who are always asking how you are doing in your preparation!)

When constructing your cards, try to incorporate many of the specific factors which contribute to your own anxiety responses. If you are uncertain about what makes you anxious and nervous before an examination, talk with a friend and share your ideas. It is often the case that sharing feelings and thoughts like this will help to sort out uncertainties in your own mind.

Some other cards which might give you some ideas:

Card 3

Two weeks before the exams, and my English lecturer is talking about the major topics which should be reviewed very thoroughly for the coming examinations. My mind is racing back to some of these topics which presently seem very foggy. There is a hushed silence in the class.

Card 4

One week before my first examination. Am looking over the examination schedule on the bulletin-board and Jim comes up and cheerily announces that the exams are not worth worrying about!!! My exam schedule shows five exams over eight days, with two on one day! Jim is still laughing and joking with some of my classmates. Somehow, I miss the joke.

Card 5

The morning of my third exam and I'm walking up the stairs to the exam room. There is a lot of nervous chatter going on amongst the other students. My mind is racing through the topics which I think will appear on the exam. I approach the door of the examination room. . .

The five sample cards should give you the general idea of how to construct your own hierarchy. Prepare about ten cards which progress from very low fear situations to the highest fear situation which you have experienced. Arrange the cards in sequence from low to high and then number them, just in case they are dropped.

How to do it

As systematic desensitization is a very important and successful method for overcoming examination anxiety, it is worthwhile to summarize and elaborate on certain steps in the process.

Relax yourself thoroughly.
- When you are very relaxed, read the first card in the sequence.
- Use your imagination to make the scene as realistic as possible. For example, if the scene is set in your room at home, glance around the room in your imagination and 'see' the furniture, the color of the walls, any pictures or other fixtures which stand out. In your imagination, sit down at your desk and feel the chair supporting your back and your legs. Rub your toes over the carpet or floor covering. If it's summer and there's a fan on, listen to its sound and feel the puffs of air blowing against your face when the fan blows in your direction. Are there any background sounds which you can hear? Radio? Television?

- Proceed through the series of cards one at a time.
- If, at any point while imagining a scene, you feel yourself becoming anxious, say 'STOP!' to yourself and picture a stop sign in your mind. The 'STOP' command will interrupt the scene which is causing the anxiety.
- Take a comfortably deep breath and say 'RELAX' to yourself as you exhale to re-establish a relaxation response. Allow as much of the tension and anxiety to flow out as you breathe out. Continue saying 'RELAX' as you breathe out until you feel thoroughly relaxed.
- Repeat the scene, experiencing the same details as you did previously. If you again experience feelings of nervousness and tension, repeat the 'STOP' command and then relax yourself.
- Keep repeating the scene until you can maintain the scene in your mind for fifteen to thirty seconds while being relaxed.
- When you have reached the point where you can maintain the scene in your mind for fifteen to thirty seconds while still being relaxed, advance to the next card and repeat the process.
- If one or more scenes prove to be particularly difficult, carry the relevant cards with you during the day. When you have a few spare seconds, imagine yourself in one of the scenes and say 'RELAX' as you breathe out. By imagining the difficult scenes over and over, you can progressively desensitize yourself to the anxiety associated with those scenes.
- By the time you have successfully worked your way through the entire hierarchy, you will find that you can relax even under the most realistically-imagined examination conditions. The secret is to pair the relaxation response which has already been associated with the word 'RELAX' to the various scenes. The process might take several weeks, but the activity (or more aptly put, the lack of activity) is quite pleasant and enjoyable.
- If you do not have weeks or even days to work through your hierarchy in a relaxed fashion, you can still benefit from spending a few minutes each hour imagining your hierarchy scenes. Carry the scenes with you and get relaxed when and where you can. Imagine one scene at a time and say 'RELAX' as you exhale. The massed practice approach is not as good as spaced practice, but it is better than going into an examination in a tight knot.

Systematic desensitization is much like taking a vaccine. You expose yourself to safe levels of examinations by using realistic imagination. If you practice over a period of time, you can attain a very positive reaction to examination anxiety.

In essence, you can take much of the nervousness out of your examination experiences by starting your review early, reviewing your notes well, learning how to relax; and by using systematic desensitization. Be certain that you start your preparation EARLY, so that you have sufficient time to master these tasks.

The purpose of starting to learn how to relax months before the examinations is to ensure that when the examinations are on, you will be able to put into practice the vital skill of relaxation. You will quickly realize that an examination room is not the conventional place to stretch out and practice your full relaxation response. However, the trained relaxer *can* call up a brief, but effective relaxation response when the stress level gets too high in the examination room. The next section describes how to use your relaxation response during the actual examination situation.

Relaxing quickly in examinations

For students who habitually have problems with strong anxiety feelings in examinations, there are many advantages in being able to relax quickly, even under examination conditions.

There are at least three reasons why being able to relax quickly in an examination can benefit the candidate. One, you are likely to be more comfortable, given that examination rooms are not generally designed with comfort in mind. Two, you can prevent muscle cramps. Writer's cramp is a common phenomenon when the muscles of the writing hand are being pushed to their limits. Three, working with a relatively relaxed mind (given the somewhat elevated level of activity common to examination conditions!) will promote more flexible thinking. You will want to be able to bend and flex you memory and recall abilities to their maximum, and hence keep your mental systems organized, but loose and working effectively.

Having stated what is likely to be obvious to most experienced examination candidates, what can the anxiety-prone person do in an examination to maintain a relaxed and flexible approach to the examination?

Keeping (relatively) relaxed in exams

- Periodically, close your eyes and take a comfortably deep

breath and then let the air out, slowly and quietly. As you breathe out, say 'RELAX' to yourself and feel the tension flowing out of your body.

- While relaxing during the deep breath, allow your arms and hands to dangle at your sides. Feel the warmth from the blood flow into your hands. Imagine the tension flowing out through your finger tips.
- Flex and relax your finger muscles several times to promote blood flow.
- Change your body position slightly to allow more blood flow to your thighs, buttocks and back. Make the movements slow and gentle so as not to disturb your neighbors.
- Stretch your arms, legs and back.
- Take another slow and deep breath and say 'RELAX' as you breathe out and then return to your work on the examination.

The entire process of breathing, dangling, flexing, changing, stretching and breathing again can be done in about thirty seconds or less. The benefits to be derived from the periodic relaxation break make the time investment very worthwhile. In order to experience the feel of the process, why not try the steps right now? Practice is the key to a better performance.

SUMMARY

Dealing with the anxieties and 'nerves' which can confront and affect most examination candidates will require an early and ardent campaign. This chapter has addressed three major issues which involve an active learning approach to examination anxiety: learning how to relax on cue; using systematic desensitization to neutralize examination anxiety; and learning how to deal with anxiety in the actual examination room. The major points are summarized below:

Learning how to relax

- Practice daily
- Establish the expectation that you will relax
- Make yourself quiet and comfortable
- Focus your attention upon your breathing
- Narrow your attention by using imagery
- Present positive and realistic suggestions to yourself
- Return to the here and now

- Chart your daily progress in learning how to relax

Using systematic desensitization to reduce examination anxiety

- Construct an examination anxiety hierarchy
- Relax yourself
- Present hierarchy scenes to yourself while relaxed
- Progress through hierarchy until the series is completed

Relaxing during the examinations

- Take periodic and brief breaks during the examination
- Close your eyes and relax your body and mind
- Stretch your limbs and shift your body position
- Check your breathing for a slow and regular rate

5
Keeping fit

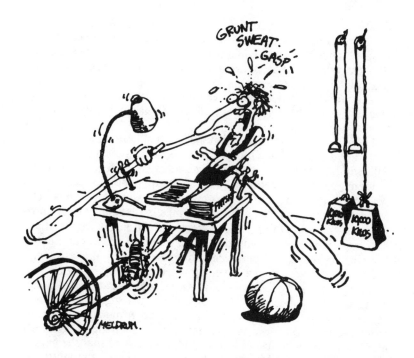

This chapter will deal with the role which fitness plays in helping you to perform to your maximum in your examinations. Few would dispute the importance of being fit for any challenging task or ordeal. While sitting at a desk for several hours might not seem to require optimum fitness, the experienced examination candidate will quickly argue otherwise. Preparing for and performing in examinations can be very demanding tasks. The weeks of intense study before the examinations as well as the high pressure which most candidates experience during the examination period are just two reasons why you should be physically and emotionally fit for your examinations.

Several very important physical fitness issues will be considered in this chapter: diet, sleep, exercise. An additional concern, emotional health, will also be discussed.

Diet

A saying frequently quoted by nutritionists is: 'We are what we eat.' A corollary of this statement might be: 'A wise person eats wisely.' These sayings highlight an important concern for examination candidates. That is, what foods should be encouraged and which avoided when examinations loom on the horizon?

Most food experts would agree that a well-balanced and diversified diet is ideal for just about all situations, including examinations.

There are certain food substances which are best limited or excluded during examination time. One, which has had a popular following among examination candidates, is coffee. In the past, students have been reputed to be large consumers of caffeinated beverages, including coffee, tea and caffeinated soft drinks. The reason for the popularity of these drinks is that the caffeine produces a 'pep-up' during those long and often late-night study sessions. However, if you drink too much of these caffeinated beverages, you can experience some very undesirable effects.

I remember very well an evening when I was reviewing for two examinations on the following day. At the beginning of the evening, I made a large beer mug full of coffee and sipped away as I reviewed. About two hours later I made another mug of coffee and, from that point on, I was in constant motion. Interspersed between many trips to the toilet, I tried to study, but found that the papers shook in my hands. My mind was a blur of frantic thoughts and finally, after several hours of very unproductive 'study,' I collapsed into bed where I then tossed and turned for several more hours.

How much coffee and tea can you drink without suffering any negative side effects? Food experts suggest that by drinking more than four to six cups of average strength coffee over a few hours, you can exceed the ability of your body to break down the caffeine. That means you will have caffeine circulating through your body, causing perhaps too much excitation.

To quantify the matter, an average strength cup of coffee contains about 100 mg. of caffeine; tea, about 60 mg. and chocolate, about 30 mg. Your body can metabolize or cope with about 600 mg.

of caffeine in a twenty-four hour period. So, do your calculations to determine how much of which drink you can have during any twenty-four hour period. Remember, going over the 600 mg. mark is likely to cause negative effects upon your concentration and study effectiveness.

A similar scenario can occur if you take stimulant pills or other self-prescribed medications. Be very careful how you use these substances, if indeed you use them at all. As a general rule, you would be wise to stay well clear of these artificial stimulants and other non-prescribed medical substances during the weeks prior to and during your examinations. Even some sedatives and tranquilizers, which are sometimes prescribed by doctors, can cause problems. While these drugs might relieve some of the anxiety problems associated with examinations, they can also produce in some people very undesirable side effects. The most important and least desirable side effect is sluggish thinking. If you have experienced excessive nervousness prior to and during previous examinations, practice the relaxation techniques described in the previous chapter. If more help is needed, consult a student counselor.

Sleep

The second fitness concern is sleep. Sleep patterns and diet can be closely associated, especially if you are drinking cup after cup of coffee or tea. However, even if you are prudent and you are limiting your caffeine intake to the levels noted above or excluding caffeinated drinks altogether, your sleep patterns are still likely to be affected during the examination period. When the examinations are drawing near and the stacks of notes are knee high, many students see the only available source of extra study time as being their normal sleep time.

If you tap this resevoir of time the night before an examination, it is unlikely that the loss of an hour or two of sleep will appreciably affect your examination performance. Many students will toss and turn during the nights before their examinations and will wake feeling nervous about the fact that they did not sleep well. Don't despair if that happens to you. Well-controlled studies have shown that critical thinking and decision-making abilities are not significantly affected by occasional loss of sleep. However, skimping on your sleep over a long period can and probably will take its toll during the examination. The major objective is to study well when you are at your desk but don't take your study problems to bed. An examination candidate needs as much rest as possible; and you can only rest effectively when you are not brooding over problems.

If you typically have had difficulty getting to sleep at night during your examination periods, then start early and practice the relaxation skills described in the previous chapter. By acquiring the ability to focus your mind on relaxing thoughts, you can actively exclude examination worries. Miraculous? No, just plain mental control. It is important to note that good mental control takes time to develop. You will need several months to work on your relaxation skills to reach the point of excluding examination worries from your mind. So, get started as soon as possible.

If you are already in the examination period and you are not sleeping well, try the following. Take a comfortably deep breath and then slowly let the air flow out. On the next inhalation, count to yourself, 'one,' and on exhalation, say to yourself, 'relax.' While saying 'one' and 'relax,' try to see your hand writing the number and word on a blackboard or, if that is too close to the examination scene, try writing the words in the sand on a quiet beach. On the next inhalation, count 'two,' followed by 'relax,' when you exhale. Continue the process up to twenty, each time saying and visualizing the respective number and words. The purpose of this exercise is to occupy your mind with a repetitive series of non-arousing words and images. If you can keep the series audibly and visually in mind, there should be little or no room left for worries about your examinations.

If your mind drifts away from the routine, add a small mechanical movement such as lifting a finger on inhalation and letting it drop on exhalation. You might find that as you progressively relax, your mind might wander and examination worries may creep in. Keep on applying the technique. Your mind will eventually drift off into a sufficiently relaxed state that sleep will come. Don't get impatient and expect instant results. Just keep the worries at bay, and bore your mind into monotony.

Exercise

The third fitness concern is exercise. As stated earlier, the examination period is no time to make drastic changes in your lifestyle, including becoming a convert to marathon running or any other popular exercize routine. But mild exercise during your study breaks can be advantageous. A brisk walk around the block, a jog to the local shop and back, or some gentle calisthenics can do wonders for your powers of concentration when you return to your books and notes.

If jogging, walking or cycling is a regular routine in your daily lifestyle, why not use one of the small walk-along tape recorders and review on the run? By recording the material you wish to review, you will actually be applying the material—reading, organizing and reciting. When making the tapes, allow for some pauses between the items for your responses. That will allow you to simply turn the recorder on and get on your way—no stopping and starting the tape.

For those examination candidates who detest strenuous exercise, you can benefit from simple stretching exercises done at your desk seat. Go on, try some. Press your palms together and then extend your arms straight over your head. Stretch them up as far as you can. Feels good, doesn't it? Now, try bending your body from side to side with your arms extended over your head. Stretch your legs out in front of you. The whole routine can be done in a few seconds and you can let a lot of tension go in that short period.

Emotional health

The approach of examinations can herald the upheaval of relationships, the failure of personal financial supports, the breakdown of motor vehicles and a number of other 'disasters.' Having counseled students over many years, I never cease to be amazed at the predicaments which students report at examination time. Students who are normally mild mannered and temperate find that an aggressive motorist has chosen the morning of an examination to pick a fight.

What to do about these dilemmas? Once again, there's no easy answer. However, if you know that you are going to be tense and a bit on the quick-to-react side, make adequate preparation before the examinations arrive. Tell your partner that you might be difficult to get along with during the next several weeks. Get your car serviced so that you can drive with a relatively restful mind. Avoid aggressive motorists on your way to the examination. Be sure to start early so that you do not provoke the anger of 'the law.' In other words, be prepared and think ahead about the possible sources of problems. Scouts are not the only people who can benefit from being prepared!

SUMMARY

Keeping fit is very important for examination candidates. However, it is far preferable to maintain your physical and emotional fitness on a continuing and long-term basis rather than convert to a zealous and new routine during the period immediately before the examinations.

Diet

- Eat a well-balanced diet
- Avoid severe weight loss campaigns during the examination period
- Monitor your intake of caffeinated beverages
- Seek your doctor's opinion about any prescribed medications

Sleep

- Try to maintain a regular sleep routine over the year
- Practice relaxation exercises if sleeping before exams is a problem.
- Do not worry about the loss of a few hours of sleep before the exams

Exercise

- Maintain a regular exercise program during the year
- Do not take up severe and strenuous exercize before the exams
- Use mild forms of exercize as study breaks
- Try simple body stretching exercizes at your desk

Emotional health

- Try to anticipate major problems during the examination period
- Warn others about the tensions you might experience
- Avoid lateness on examination days—get started early

6
Getting help early

How often have you. . .

- Walked out of a class confused and bewildered?
- Felt a rush of anxiety when a classmate has discussed a course topic with certainty and clarity and it all seemed like a foreign language to you?
- Taken every word down in class because you did not know enough about the topic to be able to sort the important concepts from the trivia?
- Avoided asking questions in class because you might appear to be 'dumb'?
- Looked over your notes and had little or no understanding

about what they meant or how they related to the topic presented in the class?

Some of the above items might be familiar but uncomfortable experiences for you. It is truly surprising how many students will plod on day after day attending classes and taking notes on material which is totally confusing. As suggested above, most of these students hope that the 'light will come on' in the next class or soon thereafter.

Just imagine the perplexing problem facing the student who has been collecting incomprehensible notes over weeks or even months. Examination time arrives and the notes are brought out to review and they look daunting and threatening. Trying to review with notes is difficult enough. Attacking a set of notes which appears foreign might be well nigh impossible, given the time remaining before the examination.

What can be done to avoid this predicament? You get full marks if you answered, 'Get help early.' This chapter will deal with the reasons why you should get help early. Having convinced you that seeking assistance well before your examinations is a good idea, some possible sources of help will be suggested. The chapter will conclude with a discussion about clarifying examination uncertainties and how to anticipate examination questions.

Seeking help

As suggested earlier, many examination candidates may shrink from teaching staff and classmates whom they see as being confident and competent. This is often because the non-confident person is making negatively-biased comparisons with these 'competent and confident' others. When these sorts of comparisons are made, the initiator is more than likely to come out the loser. No matter what the cause of the feelings of incompetence or non-confidence, there are several very good reasons why help should be sought very early.

To improve your understanding of the course content

As alluded to earlier, a very common pattern among students is to hide their notes in a safe folder week after week, and then extract them a week or so before the examinations. The gamble is that the time remaining is sufficient to untangle any difficulties they might uncover in their notes. The day of their first review arrives and 'HORRORS!,' the realization strikes them that the notes are bewildering and time simply does not permit thorough learning from the beginning. To make matters worse, it is frequently the case that an understanding of the material in the early classes is necessary to comprehend the latter topics.

To increase your studying efficiency

A recurring and very important message in this book is that a thorough mastery of the course content is the best preparation for examination success, and also the best antidote for examination nerves. However, if confusion and doubt cloud your understanding of the topics being discussed daily in class, then your efficiency rating is likely to move quickly downhill. The efficient way to handle questions is to seek appropriate answers as soon as possible and from the most relevant source.

To increase your motivation for learning

In addition to increasing your understanding of difficult concepts, taking the time to consult your teaching staff can boost your motivation in the course. You will have the chance of not only seeing and hearing how the problem can be approached from a new direction, but you will also have the opportunity to meet your lecturer on an individual basis. Sitting down and talking in your lecturer's office is potentially a far more enjoyable and instructive experience than competing for time after a lecture. You can get to know the lecturer as a person, not just a being who addresses you from a lectern.

To deal with examination nerves—early

As stated a number of times the major cause of examination nerves is late and/or poor preparation. While most cases of examination anxiety can be attributed to these causes, there are some students who are well-prepared and yet still have difficulty with severe anxiety when the assessment day arrives. If you are the conscientious student noted here and you are generally well-prepared for your examinations—but still do not do justice to your knowledge, then get help early. Considerable time is necessary to work effectively upon the anxiety problem, so do not delay in speaking to a counselor about it.

Sources of help

Having discussed several salient reasons why you should get help early and not be tempted to push the problems under the carpet, let us turn to several people to whom you can go to obtain the help.

Yourself

At the risk of sounding devious, let me say straight away that learning how to solve problems on your own is probably one of the most important lessons you can learn at any stage in your education. The process is at least twofold. Step one is to know when you have a problem. You might say that this all sounds silly. 'Who doesn't know when a problem exists?!' Lots of people. Have you ever heard the expression: 'Don't fool yourself'? The origin of the saying is probably based in the frequent experience of people choosing not to see that they have a problem. The signs of an academic problem existing in your life are the very reactions just discussed above—confusion, doubt, uncertainty, and anxiety, to mention a few. When these signs appear on a regular basis, it's time to ask yourself what is happening, or not happening. Take time to sit down and think about yourself and your progress. (Always try to be positive! 'Progress' is a much nicer word than either regression or stagnation!)

Having taken the time to sort out what is bothering you, think about how the problem can be solved. Extricating oneself from trouble can be a difficult task, and you might want to consult some reading matter on the topic. De Bono's books on problem solving are excellent sources, and recommended for those confronting personal hassles. So, take the time to try to sort out your own difficulties. If you are not successful, then try some of the following people.

Teaching staff

Your teaching staff are probably the most readily available sources of help for examination preparation problems. If, after having a brief talk with your tutor or lecturer following the class, you are still confused, then consult your textbook or other sources to clarify the concepts. In spite of your efforts, confusion might still exist. Then ask to see your tutor or lecturer individually.

As time is often limited, prepare the questions which you want to ask. Be certain to show your tutor or lecturer that you have done your work and have attempted to solve the problem on your own.

Classmates

In later years your classmates and fellow students can be valuable sources of help. Take the time to build up contacts with a range of classmates. You might try studying in a syndicate where you share your work loads and resources. A very important source of help for the student is the viewpoint of other students about the upcoming examinations. You've heard the adage: 'Many heads are better than one.' This saying has special significance in relation to examination preparation. Your skills can help others and theirs can help you. In addition to your classmates, talk to students who have studied the same subjects in previous years. They will probably be able to advise you about the content of the course and how best to go about preparing for the examinations.

One word of caution is appropriate here. Some students have a tendency to exaggerate, or conversely, to minimize the impact of their previous experiences. A year from now you might dismiss your current concern about examinations as trivial. So, when speaking to former students about their previous experiences, bear in mind that time can distort feelings and memories.

Counselors

For problems involving study skills, examination anxiety and other concerns that may affect your academic performance, contact a counselor. They have been specifically trained to deal with these problems. If your institution does not have a counselor on staff, ask one of the teaching staff or your family doctor to suggest a professional psychologist. Help is available; you just have to know whom to ask. It is also better to seek the help sooner rather than later.

Private tutors

In most large cities, you can arrange special help with a private tutor. Look under tutors or coaching colleges in the yellow pages of the telephone directory or ask your teaching staff for a referral to a good tutor. If you choose to consult a commercial tutor, compare the hourly fee rates of several tutoring agencies.

Postgraduate students

If you are studying at a college or university and are experiencing difficulties with one of your subjects, you might be able to find a postgraduate student in the department who will spend some time helping you. The help offered might be on a fee for service basis. Whether you are charged or not, it is always best to prepare for your tutorial by listing specific questions so that your time is used to its maximum.

Clarifying uncertainties about examinations

Worry and examination anxiety breed upon uncertainty. In the absence of clear information, the human mind is prone to go racing ahead, entertaining all kinds of catastrophic thoughts. The situation is much the same for the examination candidate. Uncertainty breeds anxiety and unrest.

The obvious solution to this unhappy situation is to replace uncertainty with certainty. Rather than worrying about the examination, its form, size, and content, try to determine as many relevant details as you can. Find out the who, what, where, when, and how of the exams.

The who of the examinations refers to the examiners. For most tertiary students, this question can be answered fairly easily. Your examiners will be the lecturers you have had throughout the semester or year. Candidates taking external examinations will probably not know the people who set the examination questions.

Focusing upon the former group of students, you can gain considerable insight into the examination by thinking about the strong interests and aversions of your lecturer. Place yourself in the onerous position of the lecturer who has to mark a large number of examination papers. Would you not prefer to read papers which deal with topics of personal interest? In order to locate these interest areas, go back through your notes and try to recall any unusual enthusiasm which the lecturer might have shown. You might even consider consulting the list of publications of the teaching staff to determine the special research interests of your lecturer.

What will be examined is the sixty-four dollar question. While it is very unlikely that your lecturer will spell out in fine detail the questions on the examination paper, you are nevertheless perfectly entitled to ask general questions about the examination. For example, ask whether any particular parts of the course are more important than others. It is common for the material just covered in the week or two preceding the examinations to be given less heavy emphasis than topics covered earlier.

Identifying examinable topics in a stack of lecture notes is a valuable skill which can be learned. If you make the reasonable assumption that every lecture will have at least three to five major points which the lecturer was trying to convey, then you should be able to review each lecture with the goal of extracting these major points. Note these points on a sheet of paper so that you have a list for a topic review. Of course, if the lectures are well-organized, the main points should be presented either in the initial remarks or in a summary at the end of the lecture. One way or another, try to compile a list of the major lecture points to help concentrate your review.

Another way to compile a list of examinable points is to involve your classmates. By distributing the task across a number of classmates, you make your task lighter and you benefit as well by obtaining the views of others—which might be considerably different from yours. A quality-control check at this important stage of the year can be very valuable.

A common concern of examination candidates is how widely to review. Will the examination cover laboratory experiments, suggested readings on reading lists, etc.? These are questions which you can legitimately ask your lecturer. The worst outcome of asking is that you might receive a negative response: 'I'm sorry, I can't say.' On the other hand, if you do obtain some information about the examination, you help to offset the uncertainty factor and contribute to more personal calm.

Students preparing for large-scale state or national examinations can sometimes obtain helpful information by writing to the examination administration center. Brochures which describe the types of questions and perhaps even provide sample questions are sometimes available to the candidates. (For the major international examinations such as those administered by the Educational Testing Service in Princeton, New Jersey, there are sometimes comprehensive books available to help candidates prepare for the examination.)

The *where* factor is fairly straight forward. For those readers who will be taking examinations in the classrooms, there should be no problem. However, if you are going to a different location, be it at the same institution or to another campus, be certain to allow plenty of time to find the examination room well before the starting time.

A concern similar to that of the whereabouts of the examination venues is *when* your various examinations will be held. Depending upon the size of your educational institution, you might have a provisional examination timetable published by the administration well before the examination period. This is generally done to allow students to check for any possible conflicts in the timetable. In large and complex institutions, it is not uncommon for administrative errors to be made, so that a student is scheduled to sit for two different examinations on the same day at the same time. The importance of mentioning the provisional timetable is to alert you to the fact that there might be a final timetable published just prior to the examinations. Therefore, do not assume that the provisional details are necessarily the final details. Woe be to the student who finds that the examination he has just arrived for was held yesterday!

A second reason for checking the dates and times of your examinations well before the examination period is to help you schedule your final review. If you are lucky enough to have your examinations well spaced over a two or three-week period, then you can plan your review accordingly. If, however, you face the unpleasant prospect of having four or five examinations squashed into several days, then your review schedule will look considerably different.

Now for the question of *how* you will be examined. Asking your lecturer about the format of the examination is probably one of the most helpful and least contentious issues you can raise. For instance, it is very useful to know whether you will be examined by essay, short answer, or multiple choice questions. If there are essay questions in the examination, ask how many questions you will be required to answer. Will there be a choice of, say, three out of five questions to be answered? Or will you have no choice, and thus have to answer all the questions asked? If the examination is going to have multiple choice questions, ask how many questions there will be. While asking about the types of questions, you will also want to know how long you will have for the entire examination and whether there will be any time limits for any of the sections. Once again, the more you know about the exam and its procedural details, the more relaxed you will be.

One further point is particularly relevant to the increasing number of mature-age students who are returning to study. Many students in the mature-age category will probably not have had much experience in completing a computerized answer sheet. I recall an elderly male student who became quite concerned when he faced a fairly complicated computerized answer sheet which had a series of boxes, alphabetical and numerical grids, and various blank spaces to be completed before the commencement of the examination. As he was slightly hard of hearing, he fell behind in following the instructions of the examination supervisor and therefore could not complete the identification section of the answer sheet. Rather than allow panic to set in, he wisely summoned a supervisor and asked for help. Within a short period, he was able to complete the section and start the examination with a positive bearing. Should you feel that something similar might happen to you, ask the examination supervisor if you can inspect a sample answer sheet so that you can familiarize yourself with it. You don't want to gamble on unnecessary risks when the examination day arrives.

In summary, it is critical that you obtain all the important details about your examinations early in your preparation period. Obviously, the greater your certainty about the examinations, the more composed and confident you are likely to be. If you are sitting for a local examination, know your examiner—special academic interests, research involvements, etc. Ask about what areas will be covered in the examination. Know where your examination will be held (find the venue before the examination day and check the timetable for any changes of dates or time). If possible, ask your examiners what types of questions and how many of each type will be in the examination. Be certain to obtain help before the examination if you anticipate having any specific difficulties.

Listening skills

As the quality of your examination review will depend upon the quality of your lecture notes (and of course, notes from other sources), it is reasonable to address the topic of listening skills.

Being a good listener is an active process. In fact, you might very well be working harder at listening than the speaker is at teaching. Here are some pointers on enhancing your basic listening skills:

- Be prepared to work actively when in classes.
- Preview the relevant textbook chapter before the lecture to familiarize yourself with the concepts and terminology.
- Before your lectures start, review your notes from the previous lecture to prime your mind.
- Avoid distractions by sitting in the front of the class.
- Concentrate upon the major points and be certain to record them in your notes.
- Be selective in your notetaking. Do not attempt to record everything, as a full transcription is likely to overload you, and much of the material is probably only illustrative.
- Try to leave your lectures with a basic understanding of the topics covered.
- If boredom or distractions affect you, attempt to anticipate where the lecture is going.
- Be flexible, and adapt to changes during the lecture.

Delivery cues

With your listening skills to the fore, you will next have to focus upon the speaker. Interpreting delivery cues, such as the words, phrases, pauses, and gestures of the speaker can possibly provide very helpful hints about which topics might appear on the examination paper.

Lecturers often use various vocal, postural, and visual cues to help organize their lecture and give emphasis to important points. For example, a pause in the lecture might mean that the preceding point is important, and time is being given for you to note it. On the other hand, it could mean that the lecturer has lost the train of thought. In addition to noting pauses, your eyes and ears should be sharply alert for subtle and perhaps not so subtle cues to possible examination questions. For example, if the word 'examination' is used in relation to the topic being discussed in class, lights should flash and bells should ring in your mind. Your undivided attention should then be focused upon what is being said. In addition to the word 'examination,' your ears should be alert for phrases which are likely to herald important points. A sample of phrases which should draw your attention are:

- Most importantly...
- The major point is...
- The central issue is...
- The essence of...
- It would be prudent to consider...
- The essential items on the reading list are...

SUMMARY

Performing well in your examinations means getting started early on your review and preparation. You may want to obtain help when preparing for your examinations. This chapter has presented various sources and types of help which are summarized below:

Sources of help

- Yourself—know when you need extra help by reading your own signs of uncertainty and confusion
- Teaching staff—readily available helpers
- Classmates—another readily available source of help
- Counselors—helpers for personal and technical problems
- Private tutors—helpers for a fee
- Postgraduate students—people generally who know the content and the 'system'

Clarifying uncertainties

- Know who your examiners are, if possible
- Know what major points will be examined
- Know when and where your examinations will be held
- Know the examination format—essays vs. objective tests

Enhance your listening skills

- Be prepared to work actively at listening in lectures
- Prepare the subject before your lectures so you are an informed listener
- Concentrate and understand during the lecture
- Listen with your eyes and your ears for important cues

7
Enhancing your concentration

Depend upon it, Sir, when a man knows he is to be hanged in a fortnight, it concentrates his mind wonderfully. Samuel Johnson, 1777

Concentration problems are very common to most people, but they are particulary relevant to examination candidates. The thought of being hung in a fortnight, as suggested by Samuel Johnson in the quotation above, would probably help to enhance concentration, but that is taking the matter to extremes. It is far preferable to rely on one's own abilities to control the mind.

Before starting this chapter, it might be helpful for you to consider the following statements about concentration to monitor your own level of mental control.

- After studying for several hours, you find you have no recall of the material covered.
- You have a tendency to stare blankly at your books and notes.
- You find your eyes scanning the room for interesting diversions.
- Your head pops up if anyone strolls by.
- Your head tends to nod and your eyelids fall after brief periods of study.
- You move your stack of notes from side to side and sharpen yet another pencil (just in case the other six break).
- You plan and then re-plan your present study tasks.
- You justify to yourself why trivial tasks which take you away from your desk are urgently important.
- You become easily absorbed in photos and memorabilia which are on your desk or around the room.
- You experience irresistible urges to ring friends to check for the second time the accuracy of your evening's assignments.
- You cannot refuse going to speak with a telephone caller when you are studying.
- You argue convincingly to yourself why you should watch a thirty minute television show, and then find you are still in front of the set two hours later.

Many of the hurdles which are noted above will be familiar to experienced students. As in any hurdling event or obstacle course, the experienced competitor knows the location and characteristics of the impediments. The same principle is applicable to facilitating your progress and improving your concentration powers. That is, know your own particular difficulties and then be quite persistent and do something about them.

This chapter will address the issue of faulty concentration. The first part of the chapter will deal with establishing a productive study routine, so as to enhance your concentration. The second part of the chapter will describe specific behavioral methods by which you can deal with concentration problems.

The study routine

Study time

Like many of the rituals we follow every day, effective concentration can become a firm habit. To acquire this beneficial habit, it is important to fix a daily time when you devote your full and undivided attention to studying.

For most students, the prime study time will be in the evening, with perhaps some daytime studying on weekends. While flexibility and adaptability are important qualities, equally important is the habit of effective concentration upon the task at hand. By pairing a set time with the firm expectation of concentrating effectively upon a study task, the process of studying can be considerably enhanced. For example, you might set 7:30 p.m. as the beginning of your study time. At that time you should be at your study place and getting down to work. If you use a time-activity pairing, the set time then becomes a signal for your mind to switch into gear—high gear.

In the early stages of establishing the habit of concentrated studying, set an alarm for the beginning time of your study period. That alarm is your starting signal and it is very important to get into your studying promptly when it goes off.

You can use the alarm to help build stronger and longer concentration periods. You might need to start with brief periods of concentration and progressively work up to longer time spans. For example, first set your alarm for five minutes or a shorter appropriate period. Having set the target time, keep your mind on your study task until the alarm sounds. If you have been able to concentrate for the five minutes, reward yourself with a suitable prize (e.g., pat yourself on your back) and then increase the time by one or two minutes. By using this incremental system, you are training yourself to concentrate for longer periods.

Remember, concentration is hard work, and fatigue will affect your performance. If you have worked up to a concentration period of thirty minutes, you might want to plan for a short break following the time of intensive work. However, don't be lured into taking extended breaks. Simply standing and stretching your body for one or two minutes might suffice. After three or four concentration periods of thirty minutes each, a longer break might be warranted, say ten to fifteen minutes.

To help reinforce the habit of concentration, keep a record of your progress. Make a chart on which you can plot the number of effective concentration periods which you worked through each day. You will soon see the line on the graph swooping upwards, indicating that you have acquired the ability to keep your mind on the task at hand.

When you have succeeded in maintaining your concentration for three consecutive trials at the target period, then make a new chart and increase the target time by one to three minutes. By practicing daily, you will be able to increase your concentration powers.

Study place

Just as you can develop strong study and concentration habits which become associated with the time of day, you can also adapt these habits to your place of study. That is, whenever you sit down at your desk or study place, you turn on your concentration powers. The concentration exercises described in the previous section are best applied at your desk or study place so that this particular location becomes strongly associated with effective and productive studying.

As you will be spending a considerable amount of time at your main study place, it is important that the situation be:

Quiet
Comfortable
Well-lit
Well-ventilated
Distraction-free

Of these, the first and last qualities are likely to be the most difficult to achieve. When your study area suffers from noise pollution, visual interference, or any other distraction, the best strategy is to eliminate the problem (shut the door, close the windows, draw the blinds, etc.), or move to an alternative location. Your time is valuable when you are preparing for examinations, and every five minute period counts.

Study attitude

One of the most important factors in effective concentration and productive study is a positive personal attitude about the course and subjects you are studying. We all know the psychological pain of pressing ahead with a task in which we have little or no interest. The best remedy for this problem is prevention—that is, select subjects which interest you. However, if you are caught in the situation where you are taking a required subject that repulses you, then you must deal with it—it won't go away.

Making the best of a bad situation is often a necessary survival skill of the contemporary student. How do you concentrate upon a subject that leaves you as enthused as going to the dentist for a tooth extraction? There are no easy and certain solutions, but perhaps one or more of the following might help:

- Be success-oriented—focus upon the rewards of completing the subject satisfactorily.
- Actively search for aspects of the subject that can be turned into useful information.
- Focus upon finding five central and important ideas in each lecture or reading assignment.
- Turn your study material into a mini-test by writing test questions after a study session.
- Represent the relationship between the major ideas presented in class or in a text as a geometric pattern.
- Look for ways in which you can use information from the subject in daily conversations.
- Make a list of the key terms in each subject and read them during your waiting periods each day.
- Accept a dull subject as a personal challenge and set out to prove that you can master it.
- Break study tasks up into small, manageable chores so that you can see progress in each session.
- Establish special rewards for making noteworthy progress in your problem subject.
- Wear a sweatband when you are at home studying. It can be like a welder's helmet in that you wear it to perform a specific job. The band can tell others that you are involved in your job and you are not to be disturbed.

If your situation is not just confronting one or more boring subjects but facing an entire course which is of little immediate interest to you, then see a counselor to discuss your career plans.

Concentration problem clinic

Having tried the suggestions listed above and in preceding parts of the book, it is still possible that concentration problems might plague you. Three common and persistent study problems are dealt with below:

Worry

Worries seem to bother some people more than others. While there are differences in the prevalence of the 'worrying' problem, most would agree that worrying is a counter-productive activity in that it consumes vast amounts of time and considerable emotional energy.

Worrying usually starts as a fleeting thought that flashes into your mind. 'I can't understand this! I'm going to fail!' would be a very common thought sequence for many students. Instead of dismissing these thoughts as being irrational and silly, the worrier is likely to allow them to persist and amplify. They become more and more active, leading on eventually to anxiety or depression. The entire thought sequence can be thought of as a multi-link chain, spiraling downwards. A worry is linked to an emotional reaction which is linked in turn to further worry. The whole spiraling system leads down, down, down.

How do you stop the sequence and prevent yourself from being carried down the chain into the black depths of despair? Break the second link of the chain as soon as you become aware that link number one is in your mind. Breaking these mental-emotional links is called 'thought stopping.' The technique can be applied as follows:

- An irrational thought occurs.
- Close your eyes and picture a STOP sign. See the sign flashing on and off in your mind.
- Say emphatically to yourself, 'STOP!' in rhythm with the stop sign flashing 'on.'
- Clench a hand into a fist and contract the muscles repeatedly.
- Each time you contract the muscles, say 'STOP!' to yourself.
- Repeat the process six times, taking about five seconds to carry out the exercises.
- Repeat the entire procedure every time your become aware that worrying has interrupted your concentration.

An alternative to thought-stopping is establishing a set time each day for worrying. There might be issues in your life which deserve some time for 'constructive contemplation' (a more positive term for worrying). Whenever you find yourself breaking concentration and engaging in 'constructive contemplation' about issues other than the topic you should be studying, write the worry item down.

At the end of the day, you may have a list of items to consider. Set aside, say, fifteen minutes during the evening to concentrate upon the things that interrupted your concentration earlier that day.

Worry time can also be used as a problem-solving period. You might use some problem-solving strategies or lateral thinking approaches (see the books by DeBono on lateral thinking) to sort out those worries which are amenable to solutions. After your prescribed worry time has elapsed, be disciplined and get straight back to the books. The essence of using a worry time is that you curtail the interruptions to your concentration by focusing worries into a limited time period.

Daydreaming

Daydreaming, a very common concentration hurdle, is the practice of allowing your attention to veer away from the intended topic and on to some other path. It can be a very pleasant pastime, but when examinations loom in the near future, daydreaming has to be stopped. There are several strategies you can use to prevent daydreaming and to keep your concentration going:

- Shout 'NO! NO! NO!' to yourself when you first become aware that you have been daydreaming.
- List the topics about which you have been daydreaming and the amount of time they have used.
- Stand up and turn away from your desk to reinforce the association between concentration on your studies and being seated at your desk.
- Chart your effective concentration times and post the chart in front of your desk to remind you about the necessity to maintain good concentration.
- Use reversed psychology and place a photo of your face over a picture of a sheep. Do you really want to allow your mind to be prone to wool-gathering?

Book fear

Concentration problems are often attributable to book fear, a state of anxiety which is associated with studying books, notes and any other resource connected with examinations. The fear is usually generated in the following manner. Tests and examinations create anxiety in most students. The books, notes and other study materials function as reminders about the coming examinations. The frequent association between the study materials and the anxiety creates a conditioned response whereby the student begins to avoid the study materials. The avoidance can be either physical, in which the student simply does not sit down to get started on the studying or it can be mental. The latter state of avoidance is manifest in persistent daydreaming and mental wandering.

Even though book fear can be a very well-entrenched habit and a persistent problem for many students, it is comforting to know that it is very amenable to treatment. In order to overcome the book fear and thus be able to start an effective preparation for examinations, it is necessary to consult a trained counselor very early. Early intervention will provide the opportunity to break the fear and avoidance and get you back to the work front—at your desk, with book in place.

SUMMARY

Concentration problems are very common and frequent distractors for examination candidates. Even though they are common, they can be altered by applying the strategies summarized below:

- Establish firm times and set places for studying
- Eliminate distractions from the study environment
- Foster a positive attitude towards your studies
- Use thought-stopping and a worry time to deal with worries
- Chart your effective study periods to decrease daydreaming
- Break possible fear links between books and notes and effective study
- Seek assistance from a counselor if problems persist

8
Improving your memory

Memory problems are frequently the source of student concern, especially when examinations loom in the future. Faced with a tall stack of notes and a pile of books, students are likely to begin questioning their powers to learn and remember the material. Few would dispute the role which learning and remembering play in examination success. For most students, it's just a matter of conquering these mental functions.

Learning is a complex psychological function, which for examination candidates will usually involve memorizing. Memorizing, on the other hand, entails committing the concepts, facts, figures and other material in lecture notes and books to memory. Memorizing does not necessarily mean that the material has been

72

learned, for students can memorize and then produce the material in parrot fashion without really understanding what it means. The learning process involves the process of understanding, which then enhances the ability of the candidate to recall the material and use it in an intelligent and logical fashion.

Looking at the examination process objectively, the examiners want to find out how much the student knows about certain topics. The way you convince them that you deserve to pass (and pass well) is to produce from your memory relevant and appropriately expressed knowledge—the facts, the figures, the important concepts. The central issue to most students is: 'How can I master the learning process so that the essential information can be more easily retrieved and expressed?' Perhaps you will recognize some familiar study-related issues in the following list:

- Your class notes get shoved into a folder for 'later attention'
- Review is put off until the end of the semester when the learning task will then appear to be formidable.
- Your examination preparation is typically done several panic-ridden days prior to the examinations.
- In the examinations, your mind is often plagued by confusion because you attempted to learn too much too late.
- You are disappointed when you obtain your examination marks.

If several of these experiences are familiar to you, then read on. This chapter will present ways in which you can enhance your learning by improving your memory. The principles of starting early and being systematic in your review will be discussed, followed by brief descriptions of several methods which you might use to increase your memory power.

Early review

The cardinal rule in examination preparation is to start your review early. Learning and memorizing take time and energy. Trying to cram too much learning into too little time can result in frustration and confusion. While some last-minute learning is often necessary, it is best not to depend on learning very much material the night before or the morning of an examination. Those final study hours should be reserved for consolidating the major concepts which you have already learned.

Rather than leave all of the learning until the last few days, it is far better to start your review on day one of the semester or year. Even though your mind is not going to be examination oriented at this time, it is no exaggeration to say that the examination period begins at that time.

How should you start your review? By going over your class notes each day. Before the examination period commences, you will need to have gone over your notes many times, perhaps up to five or six times in order to reach a confident level of understanding. While going through your notes, you should follow the 4R method of learning: Read, Recite, (w)Rite, Repeat. Let's look at each R in turn.

Read your notes

The initial process of reading your notes can be a difficult task. The factors which determine the quality of your notes are your note-taking ability and the organizational structure of the lectures. You will probably have to do some reorganization and restructuring when you first go over your notes. While making corrections and alterations, be sure not to re-copy whole sections of notes. Re-copying is a very time-expensive task, and most students simply cannot afford to spend time in that pursuit.

You might find that colored pens are useful to help you highlight major headings and other important points. Using an outlining approach can also enhance your learning job. That is, use A, B, C, D, etc. for the major headings and 1, 2, 3, etc. for the subpoints. In lists, number the items to help jog your memory when in the examination. If your mind responds to diagrams and charts, try to convert textual material to a visual or graphic form.

It is important to go through your notes within twenty-four hours of the lecture. If you wait beyond that time to review your notes, you will probably suffer a memory loss of up to eighty percent of the material which you did not get down in your notes but which you may want to recall. Therefore, the sooner you go through your notes after a lecture, the better they are likely to be.

Recite as you go

The second of the four R's stands for recite. Having read a section of your notes and made any necessary corrections or alterations, look up from the notes and try to recite the major points you have just read. If you cannot recite these points, go back and read through the notes again. During the recitation process, try to use the examples, charts, and graphs to help jog your memory. Any lever you can use to help recall the notes can and should be used.

Working your way systematically through your notes and pressing your mind to recall the new material is very hard work. Be aware that your mind will tire, and that your efficiency will decline. Take frequent but short breaks to allow your mind to rest. Just standing up, and stretching and shaking your arms and legs for a minute can be helpful. After two or three hours of studying, punctuated by several short breaks, you might want to take a half-hour rest before proceeding. The critical point to keep in mind when taking a break is—be disciplined. A one or two-minute break can easily be extended to thirty minutes or even an hour. Beware!

Write as you recite

The third R stands for (w)rite—allowing for some author's licence. Once you have read through your notes and mentally recited the major points, the acid test of whether you know the material is to write down the points on paper. If you can't write the points down, then you don't know the material well enough. When writing, it is not necessary to be exhaustive. That is, don't try to reproduce what you learned word for word. Use abbreviations, first letters of words, and any other shorthand that comes to mind. In addition to testing yourself, the actual process of writing is a physical application of the learned material. The more ways you can use the information you are learning, the more likely it is that you will be able to recall it later.

Repetition, repetition, . . .

The final R of the four stands for repetition. While it might sound daunting, you will probably need to go through your notes as many as five or more times. The number of repetitions will depend upon the difficulty of the material, your interest and motivation, and, of course, the amount of time available before the examinations begin.

When time is short, examination candidates have resorted to the traditional student practice of cramming. Yes, cramming information into one's head in the final days or hours before an examination can sometimes aid the otherwise unprepared candidate.

However, cramming has been found to be a poor substitute for spaced learning, or learning on a regular and long term basis. Candidates who depend upon cramming run the risk of confusion during the examination, and they are also unlikely to have any significant retention of the material in the long term. A candidate who has relied on cramming may be subject to anxiety or panic if examination questions approach the material in an unexpected way. Candidates are strongly advised to spend some time each week reviewing their class notes so that the learning process starts early, not late.

As you go through your notes, you will find that the task becomes easier. By the fifth or sixth journey, you will feel more and more satisfied and fulfilled as you demonstrate to yourself that you have a reasonable grasp of the material. The more that glow of confidence can accompany you into the examination room, the better will be the end result.

Memorizing methods

Memorizing, as suggested above, is hard work. How you tackle the task can depend upon the type of material you have to learn. There are several different strategies you might employ, each to some extent oriented towards different types of content.

Whole vs. bit-by-bit learning

There are some learning tasks which are more effectively carried out by working through the material as a whole rather than piecemeal. For example, when trying to memorize a poem or some dialogue in a play, it is generally better to keep reading through the entire text, each time trying to recall more and more of the material. Learning by wholes is easier when there is a storyline or some readily recalled continuity running through the work. Thus, when memorizing a poem, you can be aided not only by the mental pictures it suggests, but also by the poem's rhythm and rhyme. Use your imagination to bring each line to mind.

I recently heard one of my children recite the poem presented below. Read it slowly, with the aim of remembering it as a whole. Try to form pictures in your mind which will help you recall each of the lines during your first reading.

Way up North where bananas grow,

A grasshopper stood on an elephant's toe,
The elephant said with tears in his eyes,
'Pick on someone who is equal in size.'

The poem suggests some images which could help you to recall the lines of the poem. For example, the first line might evoke an image of a map with large bunches of bananas covering the northern part. The second line paints a picture of a small green grasshopper standing on a huge elephant's toe, and the third line brings forth a picture of tears flowing out of the elephant's eyes. The images of the first three lines lead up to the fourth line, which draws the reader's attention to the difference in size between the two creatures and the paradox of the grasshopper causing pain to the elephant.

You will probably find that after you have read the poem once or twice while placing these images into your mind, you will have very little difficulty reciting it. As in this example, learning by wholes is particularly well-suited to memorizing poems, speeches, and other pieces of work that have a unifying theme.

Grouping, rhyming

A second memorizing technique involves breaking down a long memory task into smaller sub-tasks. Having done this, you can then use inflection and rhyming to enhance your memory. A familiar example to many science and medical students is the memorization of the twelve cranial nerves. The task of learning the twelve nerves can be significantly enhanced by grouping them into three lots of four nerves each:

> olfactory, optic, oculomotor, trochlear,
> trigeminal, abducens, facial, auditory,
> glossopharyngeal, vagus, accessory, hypoglossal

Committing the twelve nerves to memory might be made easier if you use inflections as you repeat the words to yourself. Using inflection in this context simply means emphasizing a particular word, such as the third word in each of the three groups. Use of inflection can give a song-like quality to the series—and anything which can help fix the material in your mind is worthwhile.

Mnemonics

Mnemonics, a difficult word to spell and even more difficult to pronounce, refers to memory aids using secondary associations. Let's take the example of the twelve cranial nerves again. Instead of using the grouping and rhyming technique, you might find using the following mnemonic easier:

On old Olympus' towering top,
a fat-armed German viewed a hop.

You will note that the first letter of each word in the mnemonic sentence is also the first letter of each of the cranial nerves. By recalling the rhyme, you bring to mind the names and the order of the nerve sequence.

Mnemonics do help, but the concern of many students is that they will be able to recall the mnemonic, but not be able then to make the secondary association to the vital facts when in the examination room. The answer to this problem is to regard mnemonics only as aids. You must learn the factual material well, and then use the mnemonic to help you recall the material.

Memorizing by understanding

We have all faced memorizing tasks when we have not fully understood the background, mechanics, or theory of the material to be learned. Your experience with learning such material probably has proved to you how time-consuming learning can be if you do not understand the work.

Take, for example, learning a complex scientific process like photosynthesis. If you were to ignore the interaction of the sun, the chlorophyll, and the biochemistry of the plant cell, then trying to remember the complex assortment of facts and concepts would be a most daunting challenge. Ideally, the learning process should occur in the classroom and during your study sessions throughout the semester, but last-minute pre-examination learning is all too often an academic necessity. When faced with reviewing a complex process like photosynthesis the night before an examination, focus firstly on a general overview. Look at the major parts. How are they associated? What do they do? When you have the general picture clearly in mind, then look at the processes in more detail. Once again, break the large task into more manageable sub-tasks. This will help you to learn the material more quickly and can also give you a motivational boost by seeing progress being achieved.

Memorizing while waiting

As noted previously, repetition is necessary to fix any new material into your memory. Finding time can be a problem for many students. One way to find more learning time is to use waiting time. We all spend varying amounts of time every day waiting for things to happen—for lecturers to arrive and begin the lecture; for the bus to appear; for a friend to arrive for a lunch-time meeting. If you are prepared for these waiting periods, you can use them for review. Carry with you a packet of review cards—index cards cut to pocket size. When you find yourself waiting, pull out the cards and go through them. By reviewing your memory material in short spurts on a daily basis, you can avoid the massive learning load that can accumulate at the end of the semester. This flashcard approach is particularly helpful in learning foreign language vocabulary, key terms and concepts, formulae, and important lists. The cards are handy and can be managed easily even in rush-hour trains and buses. Why not try this system and find out at first hand how helpful it can be?

Memorizing with a tape recorder

In this era of modern technology, students are turning to tape recorders, calculators, and other electronic devices to improve their learning efficiency. A calculator can be a significant help in mathematics, and a tape recorder can be a useful aid in memory work. A cassette recorder, especially the small walk-along models with light-weight earphones, can be used for review. Instead of writing down vocabulary and key terms and concepts on flashcards, you can read the stimulus words on to a cassette tape. Leave a pause on the tape and then record the meaning of the term, word or concept you are reviewing. You can play the tape while commuting, doing the dishes, walking, or in numerous other situations where your mind is free to do some constructive learning even though your hands or body are preoccupied with something else.

Situational prompters

Another approach to using your daily time to its maximum value for learning is to pair a common daily event with revision. In other words, you say to yourself that every time you stop at a red traffic light or go through a doorway or lift the telephone receiver that you will go over a particular memory task. Thus, reviewing five vocabulary terms every time you lift the telephone receiver or go through a doorway will result in a lot of learning. The pleasant part of this process is that the review occurs in small doses during your normal daytime routine.

Using a review checklist

A review checklist is a card on which you have noted the various items which you have to learn and review. List these items down the lefthand side of the card and record the days of the present month across the top of the card. Carry the card with you each day and when you have reviewed one of the items on the card, place a small mark in the relevant box under the appropriate date. Try to go over each item several times during any one day. At the end of the day, you can see at a glance what items have been reviewed and you can then plan the next day's review.

Utilize your knowledge

After you have studied a topic, try to use it. For example, look for ways of using the information in your conversations the following day. Of course, there is a limit to the amount of time your friends will give Pythagoras's theorem when they want to discuss other more scintillating topics. While heeding the rules of social conversation, there is, nevertheless, considerable value to be gained from using your recently acquired knowledge. Perhaps creating a daily personal challenge of using material learned the day before could help motivate you.

Act it out

Although acting or miming a math formula could pose a supreme challenge even for a seasoned actor, there is no reason why you should not try to act out some more appropriate topics. For example, a poem or even the battlefield movements of the armies of a historic conflict you are studying can make the learning job easier. Caesar's Gallic Wars became for me a fascinating learning exercise because my Latin teacher brought along rubbish-bin lids (shields) and clothesline props (spears) so that the class could re-enact the classic battles. The classroom floor was not littered with blood and bones. On the contrary, it was filled with absorbed minds and attentive bodies.

Use your creative talents

As suggested earlier, memory can be enhanced by using imagery. When trying to memorize a complex chemistry formula, think about the possibility of making a cartoon or picture out of it. If you develop the ability to generate interesting images out of the ordinary, learning can take on a new dimension and your memory will improve as well.

As appropriate acronym which embodies most of the points of this chapter is ACTION.

A—apply
C—cartoon
T—try
I—imagine
O—orate
N—negate negatives, be positive

SUMMARY

A retentive and active memory will enhance the examination results for most candidates. Your memory can be improved by applying the following:

- Review early
- Read through your notes five or more times
- Recite the material you are learning
- Write brief notes to ensure you *do* know the material
- Repeat the above steps as frequently as possible
- Tailor your learning processes to the type of material to be learned
- Learn poems, speeches, plays as a whole
- Break down large and complicated learning tasks into smaller and more manageable tasks
- Use grouping, rhyming and inflection to assist learning
- Learn difficult lists by using mnemonics
- Utilize previously wasted time by having review cards, taped notes and checklists with you daily
- Apply your imagination to learning tasks using acting, drawing and other expressive outlets

9
Thinking positively

Performing well in examinations is very similar to performing well in other types of stress-filled tasks. For example, take the case of the athlete. The State championships are looming in the near future and contestants from all over the State are preparing both physically and mentally for their events. Apart from physical prowess and technical skill, what factor is likely to characterize the top performers? Having considered the title of this chapter, you won't have to stretch your imagination very far at all to guess: positive thinking.

Consider yourself and the qualities which you believe influence your outlook, especially in relation to examinations.

Do you:

- Focus predominantly upon your negative qualities?
- Compare yourself to others and find that you always seem to be on the losing side?
- Avoid asking questions in class because you think your class-mates might think you are stupid?
- React to failures and rejections by withdrawal, never returning for another attempt?
- Allow others to take advantage of you because you think you are not as good as they are?

The chances are that at least one or more of the above items will ring a note of familiarity with you. That's not because you, as an individual, are a negative thinker; it's more that we, as a society, are particularly negative in our relationships with each other. Have you noticed that the most positive compliment you hear in daily conversation is, 'Not bad!'

Looking around your own circle of friends, you probably can pick out several who you think are positive people and positive thinkers. What are the qualities in these persons which make them appear to be positive individuals? Are these persons always willing to have a go at a new experience? Are they willing to learn from their failures as well as their successes? More than likely, you have answered 'yes' to these questions.

This chapter will address the very important issue of positive thinking. In spite of the prevailing cloud of negativism which is all too frequently part of our daily behavior, decisive steps can be taken to instill more positivism in our thinking and behavior. Being positive about one's examination preparation and performance is vital. Let's look at why it is so important.

I recently saw a twenty-two-year-old technical college student who was referred to me for 'learning problems.' He started his college course at eighteen but failed totally in his first year. After working for two years he attempted his college course again as an evening student. Once again, he was unsuccessful. Reflecting upon both failures, he said he was unable to study because he kept questioning and doubting his ability to learn the material and to pass the course. He admitted thinking to himself that rather than make an all-out effort and then possibly still fail, he thought it safer to make a half-hearted attempt. That way, if he passed, well and good. However, if he failed, he could always protect his ego by saying: 'Well, if I had *really* tried, I could have passed. But I made only a minimal effort.' Failure under these conditions was easier to accept.

The mental strategy noted above is common to many students. No one likes to fail—especially if an all-out effort has been made. What are we likely to say to ourselves if we do try very hard and then fail? Most would reply: 'I'm stupid!'

Rather than fall into the trap of labeling oneself as stupid or incapable, it is far better to analyze the experience of failing in order to understand what went wrong. It could well be that other factors impeded your progress and work, and that conditions could have been better. Or perhaps your motivation for learning was low. No matter what the reasons might be, it is very important to carefully analyze each attempt, especially if you are planning to have another go at the course and examinations.

Somewhere in the distant past, I read what I consider to be a most comforting statement: 'The most successful people fail two-thirds of the time.' I could not accept that comment when I first read it, because the successful people I know seemed always to be successful. I could rarely see any hint of failure or personal doubt in these individuals.

On more careful consideration, however, it seemed to me that the reason these people succeeded was that they were always out there trying, trying, and trying again. Quite a few of their attempts were failures in strict terms, but they would probably prefer to call them 'experiences.' These negative experiences were only failures in the sense that they did not produce the anticipated results at that particular time. But were these attempts absolute failures? Definitely not! Even though the result may not have been what was hoped for, the individual was able to reflect upon the experience and to learn from it. The positive aspects could be maximized and the negative elements minimized. By positively shaping the attempts with each succeeding trial, the person was more likely to succeed in the end.

Examinations (and failure)

Why is it that failure in an examination is particularly traumatic? You might think that to enter a running race and not win is perfectly all right, but to enter an examination room and fail is another matter altogether. But is it, really? The reason why examinations are seen as forbidding experiences is that people view them as definitive gauges of worthiness—indicators of one's maximum capability.

But is that really the case? It is very important to view an examination experience in correct perspective. Yes, an examination result can be an important factor in your education, work, and personal life. For example, passing a driving test can make a great difference to your daily lifestyle. But while examinations are important, they generally are not once-in-a-lifetime experiences. If you have the misfortune to perform poorly in an examination, it is likely that you will be able to make a second attempt at a later date. I am not for a moment suggesting that a laid-back approach to examinations is best. I am saying, however, that viewing an examination as a final experience is inappropriate.

A positive approach

What can you do to help yourself become a more positive thinker, especially with respect to your examinations?

Firstly, consider what you are thinking about as you ponder an approaching examination. Thoughts such as: 'I'm going to fail!' or 'Do I really know enough to pass?' are likely to unsettle you or create a strong anxiety response and thus hinder any positive outlook. It is far better to say to yourself: 'I'll have a go at it!' or, 'I can pass!' Of course, the latter assertion assumes you have prepared for the exam and that you have a realistic chance of passing. You will recognize the hopelessness of pounding positive statements into your head if you have had little or no preparation.

A second strategy to help you become a more positive thinker is to realize that with every examination you take, you become a more experienced person. Even if some of your examination results are not the glowing successes you had hoped for, you still have the opportunity to learn something positive from your experience.

In order to get the most out of your examinations, look back carefully at your preparation period and the actual examination. Many students hide their past examination papers away, never to be looked at again. Why shun a very valuable learning resource? After all, examinations probably account for a large percentage of your final result. You can become a better examination candidate by considering the strengths and weaknesses of your past efforts.

'Did I start my review early enough?' 'Were there important areas to which I did not give sufficient attention?' 'Did I manage my time well in the examination?' Questions such as these will help focus your attention upon vital areas of learning. The object, after all, is to maximize your positive features and minimize your negative ones. After reviewing your examination papers, make an appointment with your lecturer to discuss your examination techniques. Feedback from the examiner will be a valuable resource for future examinations.

Positive steps towards examination success

- Ask yourself what is the single most interesting fact from each lecture or class.
- Place yourself in the role of the examiner. Construct three examination questions from the notes from each class lecture.
- Place a card in front of you on your desk with a meaningful positive message, such as, 'Success is the product of positive thinking.' Or make it more personal . . . 'Jeremy Wilson will study daily and pass his exams.'
- Set study goals with a close friend and meet frequently to compare your progress.
- Keep your long-term goal in mind. Make out a business card with your name and the relevant hoped-for qualifications, and look at it frequently.
- Reward yourself for thinking positively and then acting productively.
- Compile a list of topics that you did not understand in class and, after reading about them, see your lecturer. Be interested and enthused in learning more about the subject, even if you are at the same time a bit confused.
- Tell yourself to say, every time you pass through a doorway: 'I can pass!'
- Analyze your situation. If there's no real reason why you should not pass, then count on passing and work to that end.
- List your past successes and accomplishments. Believe that (with appropriate effort) your personal successes will repeat themselves.

SUMMARY

Being positive in your thinking prior to and during examinations can enhance your examination results. You can adopt a more positive outlook about your examination preparation and performance by applying the following:

- Avoid labeling yourself as 'stupid' or 'incapable'
- Consider every examination as a learning opportunity
- Challenge any beliefs about examinations being irrevocably final experiences
- Practice saying positive statements to yourself
- Study your past examination papers to improve your technique
- Boost your motivation by linking present examinations with future goals
- Consider your past successes, and realize that similar outcomes will continue with appropriate work and preparation

10
Preparing just before the examination

Even though the best time to think about preparing for your exams is day one of the year, most students probably will become painfully aware of the reality of the forthcoming ordeal some four to six weeks before the beginning of the examination period. You might see the examination timetable on the noticeboard in the hallway, or your lecturers might refer to the examination paper they are preparing. No matter what the stimulus, you are likely to respond by quickly counting the number of weeks or days or (heaven forbid!) hours before the start of your exams. If you are one of those students who have left it all to the province of luck, you might then allocate a few short periods for intense prayer. You will need every bit of help you can muster.

For experienced students, those final few weeks, days and hours are significant times. Perhaps you can recognize some of your habitual behaviors amongst the following:

- Your general pace of living increases sharply and you find that you have difficulty sitting down calmly to do some studying.
- You experience a pronounced thumping of the heart and your breathing rate is noticeably accelerated.
- You look at the stack of notes and study materials that have to be reviewed and your mind begins to feel like a mass of boiled noodles.
- Time slips away quickly and panic sets in.
- You race from one subject to another without obtaining a clear and firm understanding in any area.
- Your friends have advised you to cram, but you find that you are indecisive about which topics to cram and which to leave out.
- You find that your friends always appear to be more confident and better organized the morning of the exam.
- You frequently enter the examination room with a negative attitude.

If you have had some experience with examinations, several of the above items probably will be familiar. When you consider the pre-examination review period, you are really confronted with the issue of how to use your remaining time most effectively. Let's say you have six weeks to go before your examinations. That time will go flying by, so it is imperative to get your review into high gear as soon as possible. There are several time and organizational methods you should use so that you can get the most benefit out of your available study time.

Breaking the time barrier

In order to get the most value out of your remaining study time, firstly organize your review on several different time plans. That is, work out a weekly study plan for each of the final weeks, a daily plan for each day and finally, a study session plan for the next few hours. With these three time plans, you can see how each day's progress relates to your overall task. Every hour counts, and a quick glance at your current 'battle plan' will reinforce the necessity to keep your mind to the task and keep barreling ahead with your review.

6 Week Review Plan

Subjects	Weeks					
	1	2	3	4	5	6
A	Review 1		Review 2	Review 3	Review 4	Review 5
B	R1	R2	R3	R4	R5	
C		R1		R2	R3	R4 R5
D			R1		R2	R3 R4

Note: R = Review

The second step is to divide your study tasks into the available time. Let's say, for example, that you have four examinations of equal importance to prepare for, and you want to go through your notes and other materials in each subject about five times during the next six weeks. On an index card, rule off six vertical columns, one for each week. On the left-hand margin, list vertically the four subjects you will be reviewing. Draw an arrow for each subject across the weeks columns to the point where you plan to have completed the first review of your notes. The goals might differ depending upon the amount of material to be covered and the difficulty of the subject. Count on the first review taking much more time than the subsequent reviews. The fifth or sixth run through your notes might only take an hour or so—perhaps on the morning of the examination.

An inspection of the card shows that there are considerable differences between the subjects in the amount of time necessary for the first review of the notes. As noted earlier, review time will vary with the complexity of the subject, the amount of interest which the student has in the subject and, of course, the amount of time remaining for review. You will notice that subjects A and B have been allocated relatively brief first review periods compared to subjects C and D. The important feature of the card system is that you give sufficient time to the first review of the difficult subjects, while still having enough time to go through the notes of your other subjects. Time is certainly limited and you will have to be very careful about how you are using it. Remember, the major objective is to go through your notes several times (up to five for maximum confidence) before you enter the examination room.

Having organized the time periods for your first review, it is now essential to determine your objectives for each subject. In order to get an overview of each subject, look at the syllabus for the subject, if one is available. You should be able to list the major areas of interest or importance in each of your subjects. If a syllabus is not available, quickly leaf through your notes and divide them into logical sections. These sectional divisions can function as sub-goals you can work towards in your daily study. It is very important that you know *what* you intend to do, and how long you intend to spend on the task each time. In other words, your daily work should be *task and time specific*. If you sit down with the very general aim of 'doing some review,' you rob yourself of a valuable incentive—the feeling of accomplishment when you succeed in reaching your specific goal. Additionally, the non-specific aim of 'doing some review' allows you to become slack in your efforts. At the earliest sign of fatigue you might feel inclined to call it quits for the day, even though you have accomplished very little.

Most students know when they function at peak effectiveness. Some people are morning workers while others find they are more effective in the evening or at night. Given that you are probably going to be studying at any available hour during those final weeks before your examinations, you might want to consider what subjects you will be studying in your high and low periods. Rather than plan too far in advance, take each day as it comes and spend some time at the beginning to organize the day's work. Your mood on that day can be a factor that might well affect your study effectiveness. If you are feeling down, consider starting with a high-interest subject to get you going. When you have developed some momentum, then schedule one of your lower-interest subjects. Be flexible and adaptable, but keep the review process moving ahead. Time keeps rolling on, and the examinations are getting closer by the minute.

If your time is very limited, say five days, you may need to cut your losses and put your time where the most marks can be earned. That is, concentrate upon knowing well the material which is (a) important in the course and (b), not hard to understand. You may have to ignore particularly difficult material and topics that require considerable time to understand and learn. Trying to sort out a very complex concept when you could be consolidating easier material is just losing marks. Ask yourself where you are likely to score the most marks, and concentrate your efforts there. When time is scarce, you must be ruthlessly selective in what you do.

In summary, time will be a most pressing influence in those final few weeks. Don't become oppressed by the ever-advancing days and hours: make time work for you.

- Have an action plan for each week, day, and hour.
- Structure your review so that each session is task and time specific—you know specifically what has to be done in the set amount of time.
- Use the high and low periods of your study day to gain and then maintain momentum.

Cramming

Cramming, a traditional exercise even for the experienced student, should be seen as a last resort and definitely not as a planned stage in examination preparation. As mentioned earlier, cramming precludes thorough learning and can result in confusion during the examination. Having broached the negative side of cramming, the process does seem to be occasionally necessary and therefore some attention should be paid to how to cram as effectively as possible.

The most important element in effective cramming is to keep your mind firmly on the task of review. The very fact that you are making an eleventh-hour attack upon your notes is likely to foster thoughts of impending disaster. Allowing doubts and fears to invade your concentration is only going to waste valuable time. Admit the situation to yourself: 'Yes, I've got to cram a lot of work into a few short hours, and worrying is only going to hinder me. Now, down to work!'

In spite of your positive start, you may find worries sneaking into your learning effort. If this is the case, stand up and turn away momentarily from your desk, take a few deep, slow breaths, and then return to your study. Standing and breathing deeply—be sure to breathe *slowly*, as fast, shallow breathing can make you more tense and nervous—will interrupt the negative thoughts.

Assert your positive attack upon your review by writing on a card the words: I CAN DO IT! Place the card in front of your books and notes so that you see the words every time you glance up.

Take frequent but short breaks from your studying, as mental and physical fatigue will begin to wear you down. While you are trying to absorb a lot of work, your mind will need these short rests so that you can maintain the pace. Just getting up from your desk, walking around the room several times, and then sitting down again can be a sufficient break.

Focus upon the major points in your revision. Time is very limited, and you will have to be very selective about how you are spending it. There is no time for learning minute and trivial details. At the eleventh hour, you can expect to master or review only the major points. While going over the central ideas and concepts of your notes, try to anticipate possible examination questions. Any slight advantage you can gain at this point will help.

Keep writing down the main points as you go through your notes. The writing process helps to fix the ideas in your mind and the activity of writing can help to dissipate some of the nervous energy which can accumulate.

Read only the first and last couple of paragraphs of selected chapters *IF* you have to go back to your text books. By reading the final few paragraphs of a chapter you might find time-saving summary statements. Remember, word by word reading is very time-expensive. The night before an examination is no time to squander valuable time.

Look for the five major ideas in each lecture. Go through the entire set of notes, writing down on a separate sheet the major ideas. Don't get bogged down in detail and irrelevancies. As you extract these ideas from your lecture notes, look for common themes and associations which might be the focus of an essay question.

Beware of stimulants such as coffee, tea, and stay-awake tablets. You probably will find that your nervous system is already in high gear, and the last thing you need is additional stimulation. Too much caffeine in your body under tense cramming conditions can produce negative effects—shaking hands, faulty concentration, restlessness, and numerous trips to the toilet.

Know your sleep habits. A quick nap at three a.m. has been the undoing of many a deep-sleeping student. Under high-fatigue conditions, the intended quick nap can extend into a major sleep, even to the extent of sleeping through the alarm. Experienced examination supervisors will recount many incidents when dozy-eyed students have dashed into the examination room well after the start of the examination. If you want to take a short nap after a long night of studying, make some special provision for getting up on time. Have a friend or parent check to see that you are up, or arrange for a wake-up telephone call.

One final note about cramming. Unfortunately, there are no easy short cuts to learning a year's set of lecture notes the evening before the examination. Probably the most critical decision you should make is how much sleep you intend to go without. It is important to note that you can forfeit several hours of sleep the night before an examination without suffering any significant loss of mental functioning in the examination. The main thing is to accomplish the goals you have set yourself that night: if you go to bed satisfied that you have done your best you will be able to cope with a shortened sleep period.

The morning of the examination

Many students find that an early morning review of their notes on the day of their examination is very helpful. The purpose of the morning review is simply to run your eyes over the concepts and ideas so that the important terms are fresh in your mind when you enter the examination room in a few hours.

While your mind will be preoccupied with the examination and your review, it is very important not to overlook breakfast. Even if you are normally a piece of toast and cup of coffee breakfast person, you should consider a more substantial breakfast on your examination days. You will need sufficient nutrition in your body to carry you through two or three hours of high mental activity. Your mind should be far more active than on normal days, and your body will need extra energy reserves to deal with the additional tensions which you are likely to experience. Of course, a comfortably full stomach will avoid the embarrassment of stomach rumbles and growls which can occur if your pre-examination meal has been too light.

One crucial factor which many students take for granted on their examination day is the time it takes to travel to the examination. Most students will have been making the trip on most week days and will know the distance and time very well indeed. However, it is uncanny how often very routine matters can become inordinately difficult on examination days. Having counseled many students in distress on examination days, I can attest to the unusual frequency of traffic accidents and peculiar events which beset students on their way to examinations. In order to accommodate the unexpected, be certain to give yourself more than the normal amount of time to get to the examination room.

If you are unlucky and have an accident or experience a significant upset, or if you are ill, be certain to contact the examination authorities. If the examination is a large and particularly important one, you should consider obtaining documentary evidence about the mishap—for example, a doctor's certificate or a police accident report. The examination authority may have some provision to take into account these special circumstances when your results are being assessed or reported. The authorities will probably want some documentary evidence to support your application for special consideration.

When you have arrived outside the examination room, you will most likely find milling throngs of students, pacing about nervously. Some are clutching sheafs of notes, others are talking with simulated confidence, and still others are laughing raucously with a devil-may-care attitude. It's best to avoid them all. Those final few minutes are best spent alone in peace and quiet. Try to find a room nearby where you can sit and perhaps leaf through your notes on your own. Should another student arrive and disturb your pre-exam solitude, consider leaving tactfully; or if that's impractical, try to avoid any mind-challenging questions.

Finally, the hour will arrive when the doors to the examination room are opened and the students are asked to enter. Once again, be your own boss and enter the room with a positive bearing. If you are allowed to select your own seat, choose one where you will not be disturbed by other students who you know are restless and noisy (frequent and very audible sighs, nervous coughing, or shuffling). Give some thought to the sun's glare and heat and any other environmental factors which might affect your comfort. You'll be sitting there for several hours and you want to be as comfortable as possible.

SUMMARY

In the final few weeks before your examinations begin, time will be the most critical factor with which you will have to contend. Your preparation during this period can be enhanced by implementing the following strategies:

- Construct weekly, daily and study session plans.
- Account for differences in subject complexity and personal interest when planning your review schedules.
- Make certain every study goal is task and time-specific.
- Allocate your time in proportion to the importance of the subjects and the marks available.
- Cram only as a last resort. Spaced, regular learning is far preferable.
- Take active steps to prevent worries from impeding your studying.
- Plan to take study breaks to rest your mind, but be disciplined about time.
- Be certain to isolate the major topics in your review and learn them very well.
- Eat a substantial breakfast on examination days.
- Get started early to the examination venue to allow time for traffic problems and other unusual events.
- Should you experience illness or other problems on an examination day, obtain documentary evidence to present to the examination authorities.
- Avoid being hassled and hounded outside the examination room. Keep apart from the crowd to maintain as much calm as possible.
- Enter the examination room with a positive attitude, and find a seat location which will provide the least amount of distraction during the examination.

11
Performing well in the examination

The long-awaited day has arrived! After much sweat and toil, you will have the opportunity of showing how much (*not* how little!) you know about the topics you have been arduously studying over the past many weeks. With a good breakfast under your belt and plenty of time to arrive at the examination venue, you start off into examination day. While on the way to the examination, your mind might be entertaining some of the following concerns which relate to performing well in examinations.

- I hope I can find a parking spot near the campus.
- Is building F, the examination room location, down in the Western campus or is it amongst those new temporary buildings on the Eastern campus?

- Will I get those panicky feelings again like I did last semester?
- I hope I won't be distracted by noisy conditions similar to those which occurred last year when the builders were renovating the room upstairs.
- Those computerized answer sheets can be confusing. I wonder if we will have to use them again this year?
- I've got to be sure to read the directions more carefully so that I don't do the wrong questions this time.
- I'll try to rest my hand more often so that my handwriting doesn't deteriorate so much.

Perhaps the thoughts suggested above seem like a potential disaster area for an examination candidate. However, the issues are important and certainly worth your attention. Examination days carry more importance than most other days in your academic year, so you want to be as fully prepared as possible, both academically *and* practically. This chapter will discuss some of the issues which warrant your attention and serious consideration before and during your examinations.

Verify the venue

As suggested above and mentioned briefly before, it is very important to verify the exact location of your examination. In some large educational institutions, your examinations might be held in locations unfamiliar to you. When consulting the examination timetable before the examination period begins, take time to locate the exact venues for each of your examinations. You should not only find the buildings, but also the precise rooms. In spite of the reputation for logical thinking and planning for which educational institutions have been respected, it is not uncommon to find that rooms do not necessarily run in numerical order or that buildings are known by only one name. Don't wait until the morning of an examination to sort out in your mind any confusion about the venue.

Check-in time

Depending upon the type of examination for which you are sitting, you will want to be certain about the correct arrival time. For particularly large examinations, there might be a specified arrival time which allows for checking-in of the examinees. It may sound unduly complicated and potentially paranoiac, but in some examinations such as those which qualify candidates to work overseas, the check-in procedure may involve checking of passports and even handwriting specimens. It is important to arrive at the specified arrival time so that you don't feel rushed and thus prone to anxiety.

Seating

The issue of examination room seating was raised briefly in the preceding chapter, but as you will be spending considerable time in your examination room seat, the matter warrants reiteration. On entering the examination room, you will either be assigned a seat or you will be able to select a seat. If the latter is the case, several considerations could be pertinent. Firstly, if you have found that in previous examinations you were distracted by students sitting around you, you might want to select a seat in the front of the examination room. While you possibly will have students sitting beside you, the bulk of the students will be behind you. The only problem in sitting at the front of the examination room is that you could be distracted by the supervisors, who generally pace about the room.

Having decided whether you prefer a front seat or one somewhere else in the room, you might next consider the temperature factor. If you are sitting for your examinations in the warm months, take note of the window locations and the angle of the sun. If the room is already warm, it will become warmer still when the area is packed with other candidates. Therefore, avoid seats where you will be bathed in sunshine. If you are assigned a seat in a sunny spot, ask the supervisor if the blinds or shades can be adjusted to prevent discomfort from either the heat or glare of the sun.

Just as personal accidents seem to occur more frequently on examination days, the council road workers seem also to choose these days to tear up the pavement outside examination rooms. Trying to divert a team of council workers from their appointed duty for the day is a hopeless task. If you have the misfortune to strike this situation, it would seem that your only recourse is to close the windows and draw the blinds or curtains in order to muffle as much noise as possible. If the noise is a major distraction, be certain to mention your concern to the supervisors. In large examinations, provision is generally made for the supervisors to report these sorts of irregularities to the administrative center.

Answer-sheet identification

In examinations where computerized answer sheets are used, time will be allowed at the beginning of the examination for the candidates to complete identification grids on the answer sheets. In order to complete this procedure fully, you may be asked to record a registration number (that is, if pre-registration was necessary to sit for the examination). Be certain to have your registration slip when you leave home for these examinations.

In addition to a registration number which you may be asked to produce, you will certainly have to provide your name and possibly other information, such as the correct name of your academic course, your institutional affiliation, your date of birth, examination center number, and date. The whole process can be confusing and the matter is not made any easier by having to fill in numeric and alphabetical grids. The major problem to guard against is filling in the right letter, but in the wrong column. This problem is more likely to occur in the number grid where many students assume that the number zero is the last number in the vertical columns instead of the first number. Given that you are most likely to be firstly identified by your student or registration number, filling in the wrong number can cause all sorts of difficulties. It is always best to check that you have filled in the correct letters and numbers after you have completed the grids. Should you make a mistake, be certain to erase the error completely and fill in the correct space.

Reading the examination directions

A critical step in any examination is reading, and then re-reading the directions. Re-reading the directions is definitely *not* a waste of time. Many students have ploughed into their examination papers with only a once-over light reading of the directions, and then discovered too late that they have made a fundamental error in how to complete the examination.

I vividly recall a philosophy examination in which I frantically dashed through two essays of the three presented in the paper and then went on to the short answer and multiple choice parts of the examination. I walked out of the examination only to find from my classmates that the instructions required only one of the three essays to be completed. The twenty or thirty minutes I had spent pushing my pen through paragraph after paragraph on the extra essay could have been spent considering the short answer and multiple choice questions at a more leisurely pace. Of course, I received no extra credit for the additional essay. If anything, the marker probably was a bit perplexed. In retrospect, I had made the mistake because I had been accustomed to doing two of the usual three questions presented in previous essay examinations. The instructions to do only one question made little impression on me because of my well-entrenched expectations. The moral of this experience is to read the directions at least twice, and very carefully.

Reading time

Following the initial formalities, you might be given a short time to read the examination questions. During this period, students are generally not allowed to do any writing. The reading time is intended to allow you to read and think about the questions. However, the initial exposure to the examination questions can produce quite strong reactions in your mind. Imagine yourself reading the first question which deals with an issue you thought was trivial and therefore treated very lightly in your review. What sorts of feelings are likely to be pulsing through your body? Probably strong fear, if not sheer panic. Many students might become extremely tense and begin to entertain thoughts of impending failure. Before you allow a Doomsday attitude to set in, move along to the next question. Here you may well find that your preparation will be more fruitfully rewarded.

Having read the instructions and the examination questions, you can establish your plan of attack. Knowing the number of questions and their focus, and perhaps their differential mark value, you can then allocate your time and your priorities.

Time allocation

Allocating your time to the major section or questions on the paper takes only a minute or two and is a simple task to complete, but many candidates go flying past this critical step in their haste to start writing. Many of these students are the ones who write notes to the markers in the final minute of the examination: 'I ran out of time and could not complete this question.' Such notes win very little sympathy from markers, and certainly no marks. Part of the examination process is to hold yourself accountable for the way you use your time. Hence, take a minute or two at the start of the examination to get yourself organized.

How do you apportion your time in an examination? As a basic principle, you want to be certain that you obtain credit for the material you know. You can imagine the frustration of working through the examination questions in their presented order and finding that you do not have enough time to fully complete the last question, an item addressing an area you know particularly well. In order to prevent this situation from occurring, list the order in which you intend to do the questions at the beginning of the examination. The order should take into account two major criteria: your knowledge of the questions and the mark-value of the various questions. Having decided how much time you plan to devote to each question, it is up to you to keep to the plan. Remember, it is far better to have something down on paper for each question than have a near perfect answer for one question and empty space for the other questions.

Another consideration which might be relevant to your time allocation is your possible preference for essay, short answer and multiple-choice type questions. Some students have reported that because they felt they were weak in essay writing, they devoted too much time to the essay part of the examination and consequently did not have enough time to deal with the multiple choice questions. Once again, be certain that you get credit for your strengths. The following chapter will discuss the different types of examination questions.

One further consideration when planning your attack is fatigue and writer's cramp. If you have the option of writing several essays and completing a series of multiple choice questions, you might want to do one or two of the essays, switch to the multiple choice section, and then return to complete the essays. By inserting the multiple choice section in the middle of your examination, you allow your hand to have a bit more rest. Not only will your hand get a break, but your mind can also benefit by switching from the creative task of composing essay answers to the more direct function of deciding which of the multiple choice alternatives is the best response. Generally speaking, giving yourself a change of pace during examinations is a good idea. Staying in the same mental gear can result in undue fatigue.

One final point is well worth mentioning. In some large public examinations, there might be restrictions upon going back to previously completed sections of the examination. The instructions should clearly specify any such restrictions. Be certain to listen carefully and consider these special conditions when you are planning how to proceed with your examination.

Neatness

As noted above, after several hours of writing, your hand can get tired and your handwriting can deteriorate. Look over some of your past examination papers and see if your writing was legible. If your writing is indecipherable (you might want to have a friend pass judgement), practice writing for long periods to condition your hand muscles. Can you imagine a marathon runner not spending considerable time preparing his or her muscles? The analogous situation applies to the hand muscles of examination candidates.

The reason for improving your handwriting is quite simple. Clear and legible writing can win you marks. Most examination markers have to read paper after paper and if they strike a series of almost indecipherable essays, the marker is not likely to be sympathetic to the plight of the fatigued candidate. Make the situation as easy for the marker and as beneficial for yourself as you can.

Checking your paper

Just before the end of the examination, take a few minutes to look over your answers/essays with the purpose of correcting spelling errors, inserting punctuation marks which might have been overlooked and generally tidying up your paper. If you have used a computerized answer sheet, be certain that you have not left any stray marks, for these can possibly be read as answers by the scoring machine. Once again, taking the time to rectify spelling errors and grammatical mistakes is worth the few brief minutes.

These errors can give an examiner an unfavorable impression of your knowledge and capabilities.

SUMMARY

It is vital that you complete correctly the identification part of the examination. Following the identification procedures, the reading time provides a valuable opportunity not only to collect your ideas about the essay questions, but also to plan your examination strategy. Factors such as the difficulty of the questions, the strength of your preparation, the types of questions, and the time constraints are important considerations. In order to use your time effectively, you must remain calm, organized and disciplined. A well-planned strategy will help to keep you on the path to success.

The value of many weeks of hard work can be compromised by some unfortunate oversights on examination day. The following suggestions should be applied on examination day to ensure that you obtain the best possible outcome:

- Be certain to locate the building and room where your examinations are to be held before the day of each exam.
- Arrive sufficiently early to allow for check-in procedures.
- If given the option, choose a seat in the examination room which will maximize your comfort and avoid any anticipated distractions.
- Notify a supervisor about any significant noise or other distraction which might affect your performance.
- Familiarize yourself with the format and instructions of the computerized answer sheets (when relevant) if these are new to you.
- Read the examination instructions twice and underline any key words.
- Plan the order in which you will answer the questions during the reading time.
- Allocate time to the questions and sections of the examination to maximize your strong points and to ensure you obtain credit for the material you know well.
- Practice your handwriting under simulated examination conditions to improve the legibility of your writing, if this is a problem.
- Correct any spelling and grammatical errors at the end of the examination.

12
Dealing with particular types of examinations

You, as the examination candidate, are faced with the daunting task of confronting a variety of different examination formats. You might have to demonstrate your logical reasoning and creative abilities in one or more essay questions; or show how well you can condense a series of logical thoughts into one concise paragragh in a short answer section; or cope with multiple choice questions.

A common misconception held by many candidates is that examinations are failed because the candidates did not know the material sufficiently well to pass. While knowing the material is important, a far more important criterion for passing examinations is the candidate's ability to think and argue in a logical, concise and clear way. Clear and concise expression is obviously more important in essay examinations than in multiple choice tests. However, you will certainly have to have a clear and logical mind to work your way through a battery of complex multiple choice questions.

This chapter will address the major types of examinations, including essays, short answer, multiple choice, true-false, and matching. A recent and interesting variation in examination format has been the open-book examination. On initial impression, the uninitiated might think that taking one's books and notes into the examination is the proverbial piece of cake. Not so! Finally, the important issue of the laboratory examination will be discussed.

Essay examinations

Writing essays under examination conditions has been a traditional method of assessment for more years than most educators want to remember. The assumption behind the essay examination is that sitting in an examination room pushing your pen and prodding your brain for two to three consecutive hours is a valid way to measure your academic merit. This might or might not be so. The reality is, however, that essay examinations are very common and you are well advised to be prepared for them. This section will present some guidelines which will assist you in performing as well as possible in examination essays.

Read and interpret the question carefully

The first and foremost task in answering an essay question is to be certain you understand what is being asked. That might sound simplistic, but hasty reading and misinterpretation of the question have been the undoing of many a candidate. In order to assist you in understanding what specifically is being asked, read the question, then re-read it, and then underline the key words.

Underline the key words

The key words in the essay are the topical terms and concepts about which you are being asked to write and the operational words which tell you how you are to do it. The following list presents some common operational words found in questions in essay examinations.

Analyze—means to describe the main ideas and their relationships, assumptions and significance.

Compare—means to show the pros and cons or the similarities and differences.

Contrast—means to compare by focusing upon the differences.

Criticize—means to present your considered opinion based upon the pros and cons. Criticizing does not necessarily mean condemning the idea. It is best to present a balanced argument showing both the positive and negative points.

Define—means to present the meaning of the term, generally in a formalized way. Including an example will enhance your definition.

Describe—means to present a detailed and accurate picture of the event or phenomenon.

Discuss—means to describe the event or phenomenon, but giving the positive and negative aspects. At university level, it would be fair to expect a critical discussion, citing the significance and assumptions, if relevant.

Evaluate—means to weigh up or give your assessment of the relevant matter citing positive and negative features, advantages and disadvantages, etc.

Interpret—means to present the meaning using examples and presenting your opinion.

Justify—means to present the basis for a particular event or phenomenon and why you think it is so. You will be expected to present evidence to support your views and conclusions.

Review—means to present a summary of the important aspects or parts and comment critically where appropriate.

Summarize—means to present a brief overview of the major points with commentary about why they are important.

Trace—means to describe the history, development or progress of the event or phenomenon.

Write down your initial ideas

Having read the question and underlined the key words, jot down immediately the ideas which come to your mind. Don't worry about the quality of these ideas, just get them down. The process is similar to brainstorming, a process of getting ideas out, no matter what their quality. It's quantity you want at this stage.

Organize your ideas

After you have brainstormed the essay topic for several minutes, look for central themes or connecting thoughts which relate the ideas to the essay topic. Pay particular attention to the instruction words, such as 'critically discuss,' 'evaluate,' etc. They will help you structure your essay.

Let's take an example to help make this point clearer. Imagine that you have been asked the following question in an economics examination: 'Compare and contrast the economic theories of Marx and Keynes, with special reference to the national economic situation over the past two years.' Having jotted down ideas relevant to the theories of Marx and Keynes, choose those which have special relevance to the economic conditions over the past two years. Try to organize your ideas into a simple and logical structure, perhaps using geometric figures or other graphic forms to assist you in the organizing.

Outline your essay

Having jotted down your ideas and major points and tried to organize them in a coherent and logical structure, take perhaps five minutes to carry out the next and very important step—writing an outline. In the introductory paragraph, remember that you must introduce the topic and, just as importantly, you must tell the marker how you will be structuring the essay. The succeeding paragraphs should deal with the major points you are trying to establish in your essay. If you are in doubt about what to say, ask yourself what are the five most important aspects of the topic being asked and then try to link them together in some kind of relevant structure. Having outlined the introduction and body of the essay, devote a paragraph or two at the end to summarize your argument and present your conclusion. The importance of preparing an outline before you start really addresses the problem of digression, straying from the central theme of the essay. In a time-limited exercise like an examination, it is critical that you plan your essay and then stay on target. Make sure you stick to your time allocation *strictly*.

Writing your essay

With an eye on the clock, you are now faced with the task of writing your essay. As specified before, keep to your time schedule so that you can attempt all the questions. When writing your essays, there are several guidelines which might be helpful.

- Get directly to the point.

In the first paragraph, tell the marker what you are going to say and how you are going to present your argument. The introductory paragraph below might be appropriate for the Marx and Keynes question mentioned earlier:

'The theories of Marx and Keynes have continued to have an impact upon current economic conditions. This essay will firstly present a brief synopsis of Keynesian and Marxist theories and then present the positive and negative aspects of each theory, especially as they relate to five current economic phenomena: A, B, C, D, and E. Each of these phenomena will be critically analyzed with reference first to Keynesian theory and then to the theory of Marx. The essay will conclude with a statement about which theory appears to have the more practical value for the national economic situation over the past two years.'

The marker who reads the introductory paragraph will probably respond with pleasure, relieved that the essay seems to be well-planned and organized. By getting directly to the point and showing the marker how you are going to progress, you are establishing a most favorable impact.

• Focus upon the major points you are trying to present.

Having introduced your argument and how you are going to handle it, try to deal with each of your major points in one paragraph in the body of your essay. Each point can be presented as the lead sentence of the paragraph and the following sentences can be used to help illustrate or amplify the point.

• Use transitional linking phrases.

To help the marker follow your presentation and argument, it is useful to employ transitional linking phrases to make your essay flow more smoothly. The transitional links can also serve as guideposts, telling the marker what you have completed and where you are going next.

Take, for example, the following part of a sentence midway in your essay: 'Having considered the current economic phenomena A and B, the present situation C can be regarded as. . .' The transitional phrase at the start of this sentence tells the reader that you have completed points A and B and that you are now progressing to C. By using these transitional phrases, you make the marker's job easier and the easier you make the work for the marker, the better you are likely to fare in the examination.

• Use the marker's language.

As suggested earlier, your marks will not only depend upon how much you know, but also upon how you present your essay.

The concern for your presentation can be focused upon several levels of your essay: at the overall organization of your essay; at the structure of your paragraphs; and even further down to the level of the actual words you choose in your sentences. Does that sound too pedantic? Perhaps, but ask any accomplished marketing or advertising person and they will confirm the importance which language plays in marketing a product—in the present case, you are trying to market your essay.

One strategy respected by most experienced salespeople and marketing experts is that of adopting the language of your client during the transaction. This principle can be transferred from the commercial sector to the ivory towers of academe. For example, if your examiner customarily uses expressions such as 'an analysis of the assumptions shows. . .' or 'a critical appraisal of the implications suggests. . .'; or 'the validity of the assertion appears tenuous because. . . ,' then use the same sorts of terms and phrases in your responses. Be careful, though, not to take this process too far—merely copying someone else's style is not an automatic recipe for success.

• Summarize your argument using the phrasing of the question.

At the end of your essay, you will want to summarize your argument. A helpful way to insure that you are still on target is to use selected phrases from the question to once again firmly establish in the marker's mind that you have addressed the topic in an organized and cogent way.

Checking your essay

Having finished writing your essay, you should briefly re-read it to check for spelling errors and grammatical mistakes. You might also discover ambiguous sentences and phrases which can be quickly remedied. Be certain that you keep your essay neat and legible. The best essay in the class will suffer if it is virtually indecipherable. Remember, your marker is faced with the daunting task of reading many, many essays. Should your essay happen to be in the last pile and also be sloppy and unreadable, imagine how the marker will react.

Attempting every question

Make every attempt to write something, even if you *think* you know nothing about the essay topic. Many students make the mistake of giving up too easily when they strike a question which appears to be beyond their ability or comprehension. The simple truth of the matter is that absolutely no marks whatsoever can be awarded for empty space. Even if you cannot substantiate an argument in an essay with relevant facts and details, list in a logical fashion the major points which you think are most applicable. You might get nothing, but then a sympathetic or perhaps a bleary-eyed and fatigued marker may give you a few marks for your effort. When it comes down to the final tally, a few marks are better than nothing at all.

Practicing your examination essay-writing skills

The emphasis in the preceding section has focused upon being logical in your thinking and organized in your writing. These are very worthwhile qualities to have, but you are probably asking: 'How can I become more logical and more organized in my examination essays, especially under the gaze of the supervisors and the pressure of the clock?' The answer is, *practice*. If you have had very little prior experience with examinations, try reading the examination papers of past years, especially those written by accomplished students. If past papers are not available to read, try practicing your essay-writing skills. Ask a classmate to compose several questions for you. In a spare classroom, write the essays under the same time limits and conditions which you will have in the real examination. Your classmate might help even further by reading your responses and giving you some constructive comments.

The short answer examination

The short answer examination can vary from asking you to complete sentences with short phrases to writing several paragraphs on a specific topic. Taking the name of this type of examination literally, the object is to be concise and brief in your responses. If you are asked to write several short paragraphs on a topic, you can generally view the exercise as being a mini-essay. Apply the principles set out in the preceding section, but limit the amount of space you give to examples and illustrative material. The examiner is wanting to find out what you know, so get straight to the point and don't waffle.

The multiple choice examination

There has been a very marked rise in the use of multiple choice examinations in recent years. The popularity of the multiple choice format is most probably explained by the ease of marking and analyzing the results using computerized answer sheets. Once a collection of questions has been developed, the examiner can sit back and wait for the results printout. It sounds easy, but the time saved in marking is generally taken up in developing clear and non-ambiguous questions. From the candidate's perspective, multiple choice questions can cause anxiety, fear—even panic. Most of these candidate reactions are due to faulty preparation. However, some students find the multiple choice format to be confusing and perplexing. This section will present some guidelines to help you prepare and perform in multiple choice examinations to the best of your ability.

Preparation

Most candidates who have experienced the rigors of multiple choice examinations will readily admit that they must know their study materials very thoroughly. Unlike the essay format where you might have a choice of questions, and where you can explain your ideas, the multiple choice examination is far more restrictive and decisive. There is no opportunity for explanation—you are either right, or you are wrong. There are no in-betweens.

Your preparation for multiple choice examinations is best done on a systematic and daily plus weekly basis. Plan to go over your notes many times—up to five to six times to have the facts, figures, dates and concepts firmly fixed in your mind. It is not sufficient to be just familiar with your notes and study material; you must know the material well enough to write it down. If you can't write it down, you simply do not know it well enough! For a more detailed discussion about how you can systematize your review, consult Chapters One to Three of this book. In addition to knowing your study material, you will also want to know as much as possible about the examination—number of questions, differential weighting of the examination sections, special conditions, etc. Ask your lecturer about these examination considerations and ask former students who sat for the examination about their experiences.

Starting a multiple choice examination

If your multiple choice examination involves a computerized answer sheet, you will initially be asked to complete the candidate identification grid. Consult the section in Chapter Eleven (page 100) about how to complete these identification grids.

The next important step before beginning to answer the questions is to read the directions very carefully. Pay particular attention to the layout of the answer sheet so that you do not commit the very common mistake of recording your answers in the wrong answer spaces. Many students in multiple choice examinations have found towards the end of the examination that they are one question out. That is, they find that they have been recording, for example, the answer to question 81 in the space for answer 80. Should you discover that this mistake has occurred, summon a supervisor and ask what should be done. You might be offered a chance to re-align the answers after the test booklets have been collected at the end of the examination.

Working through the examination

In order to do justice to your preparation, there are several guidelines which might be of help to you in multiple choice examinations:

- Be certain to fill in completely the answer spaces.
- Erase completely any errors.
- Be sure not to mark two answers for the same question. The marking machine is generally programmed to mark automatically any such response pattern as wrong.
- At the risk of being repetitious, be certain that you record your answers in the correct answer space.
- Work rapidly, but carefully, through the examination and do the easy questions first.
- Mark the questions you want to reconsider but be careful not to have such a mark confused with an answer.
- Make marginal notes in the test booklet for later consideration.
- Underline key words in the test booklet. Words such as all,

many, some, none, always, sometimes, never, more, less, best and least are a sample of key words which can help you to interpret the questions.

Reconsidering questions and changing answers

The issue of changing answers in multiple choice tests has been studied carefully. The outcome of these studies suggests that if you have a good reason or a strong hunch that another answer choice is more correct, then change it. The results of the studies show that candidates who change answers using these criteria are twice as likely to change an answer from wrong to right as they are to change it from right to wrong.

Guessing

If you have followed the advice of this book, you will have previously determined whether you are penalized for guessing. If there is a built-in penalty system for guessing, then you might be eroding your final mark by guessing on questions in which you are in doubt. On the other hand, if there is no penalty for guessing, you are throwing away a one in five chance of getting a correct answer for every item you leave blank. If you have no intuitive feelings about the question, and all five options appear to be equally plausible (meaning you don't have a clue about the answer!), then you have the problem of selecting between choices (a), (b), (c), (d), and (e). For what it is worth, you might answer (b) to all such questions. The rationale for this choice is that (a) and (e) are too extreme; (c) is too average; and (b) is closer to the beginning than (d). If you can argue convincingly for another answer choice, then use it.

Cheating

The advent of the multiple choice examination seems to have prompted the development of exceedingly accurate long-distance visual acuity amongst examination candidates. What that means in plain English is that multiple choice candidates have been tempted to read the answer pattern from their neighbor's paper (assuming, of course, that their neighbor is considered to be a brighter and more knowledgeable student).

Examiners have been quick to counter this problem of visual

plundering. They have developed not only parallel versions of the examinations, but also printed the answer sheets in both vertical and horizontal formats in order to deter or confuse would-be cheaters. In addition to these obstacles, there is also the ever-roving supervisor who is observing the head and eye movements of the candidates. Rather than risk a very embarrassing incident and possibly damage your future career, invest your time in a thorough preparation for the examination. Therefore, forget about cheating. Aside from the moral implications of cheating, you might find that your classmates are far less knowledgeable than you.

Checking your answer sheet

Shortly before the end of the examination, save a short amount of time to check your answer sheet to see that you have recorded your answers correctly and fully. Erase any stray marks on your answer sheet, as these could be read by the marking machine as answers. Finally, check to see that you have recorded your candidate identification information correctly.

True–false examinations

As multiple choice examinations have become more popular, the true-false examination seems to have become less frequently used. Perhaps the explanation is that the multiple choice examination is really at core a true-false examination, but it allows the examiner to assess the knowledge of the candidate more exactingly. In responding to true-false questions, the same principles which were discussed in the previous section can be applied. The candidate should pay particular attention to the wording in the questions and should underline the key words. As there is a 50 per cent chance of guessing correctly in true-false examinations, it is often the case that a penalty is applied. Be certain to find out before you start the examination if this is so.

Matching questions

Matching questions generally appear as two columns of terms and the candidate is asked to match each term with its most correct counterpart. When confronting matching questions, read both columns quickly to obtain an overview of the items. Then consider the items in the left column which you think you know and look down through the right column, searching for the most appropriate match. When you have completed the easy matches, then consider the remainder. If you get stuck, try working in the opposite direction. That is, think first about the remaining items in the right column and look for the most appropriate match in the left column. If you have several unmatched items at the end, guess unless you have been advised not to because of an inbuilt penalty for guessing.

Open-book examinations

A recent variation in examinations is the open-book approach. With this format, candidates are generally allowed to bring their books and their notes into the examination room. At first thought, an open-book examination might seem to make examination preparation redundant. Not so. Enticing as the concept might be, the open-book examination requires the candidate to know the material as well as for an orthodox examination. You must know the major topics, their associations and, if necessary, the location in your notes of supporting material. There is generally not sufficient time to go back over notes and books to extract the major ideas and facts during the examination.

The only advantage for the student is that specific details can be checked. Instead of learning twenty formulae and exhaustive lists of data, know where they can be quickly found in your notes and books. However, be certain that you cover the other material just as thoroughly as you would for a regular examination. The disadvantage of an open-book examination is that the examiner might expect a higher quality of product because of the concession. To reiterate, do not be lulled into a feeling of false confidence with this format. Prepare just as thoroughly as you would for a regular examination.

Laboratory examinations

For science-oriented students, laboratory examinations can present challenging assessment experiences. In the medical, biological and geological sciences, these examinations might take the form of 'musical chairs.' As you can guess, there is no music and there is no party atmosphere. There is, however, a progression of students moving from specimen to specimen or from microscope to microscope. The task is generally to identify the tagged or marked part, or perhaps the whole specimen. You may also be asked to answer specific questions relating to the tagged material. As you have a strict time limit before you have to move on to the next station, the pressure can be intense.

When preparing for these examinations, you will want to have thoroughly examined the complete range of the laboratory material. It is very important to examine as many different specimens as possible so that you are familiar with the variations which normally occur. When preparing for the examination, move the specimens around so that you are familiar with the different perspectives. Take note of differences in color, texture, shape and size. The more familiar you are with the specimens in your laboratory group, the better. Study with some classmates and ask them to set up some specimen tests for you. It is important to take note of any unusual features which your examiner might think will separate the superior candidates from the rest.

A few practical suggestions for those students undertaking microscope examinations. Do not touch the slide or specimen under the microscope unless you are allowed to do so. If you think that a specimen has been jarred and the pointer is wrongly positioned, summon a supervisor immediately. If you wear glasses, be certain that they are clean. It's no time to have foggy vision. If you have skipped any places on your answer sheet, be certain that you record your answers in the correct places.

Laboratory practical examinations require many hours of preparation in the laboratory. As the laboratory may be open for only a few hours a day, it is very important to prepare and review on a regular basis throughout the semester. If you leave your review until the final few days, you may find that there simply is not sufficient time to prepare adequately. You will also find that you have to compete with other students for access to the specimens which you want to examine. It's far better to look upon the final few days as an opportunity to tie up loose ends and consolidate the material in your mind.

SUMMARY

Examinations vary greatly in format, style, procedures and even setting (from the large hall to the laboratory). Candidates preparing for their examinations should ask what types of examinations they will be confronting so that their preparation is specific to the format. The major features of the standard examination formats are summarized below:

Essay examinations

- Read and interpret the questions very carefully.
- Underline the important words in the question to focus your attention.
- Jot down your initial ideas—the more the better.
- Try various organizational ideas which link the salient ideas together in the most logical and concise way.
- Outline your essay based upon your organizational scheme.
- Write your essay, paying close attention to the logical development of your argument and to the flow of your prose.
- Keep the reader of your essay informed about the path and progress of the essay by using frequent transitional phrases.
- Check your essays at the end of the examination period to correct spelling and grammatical errors.
- Practice your essay-writing skills under simulated examination conditions if you question your ability to perform well.

Short answer examinations

- Consider short answer examinations to be tests of concise and logical thinking.
- Apply the same principles as for essays, but limit examples and superfluous explanations.

Multiple choice examinations

- Prepare very thoroughly with attention paid to important details.
- Be certain to complete correctly the identification section of the answer sheet.
- Do the easy questions first and return to the harder ones later.
- Change answers if you have a strong feeling that your first response was wrong.

- Guess only if there is no penalty for doing so.
- Don't cheat.
- Take care that every answer is being recorded in the correct space.
- Check your paper at the end of the examination for stray marks which may be confused with your answers.

True-false examinations

- Be cautious about guessing, as penalties are generally applied.
- Underline key words in the questions.
- Apply the same principles as in multiple choice examinations.

Open book examinations

- Know the major topics and concepts as you would for a regular essay examination, but know where to find supporting details in your notes and materials.
- Be aware of false confidence just because you have your notes with you.

Laboratory examinations

- Carefully examine the complete range of laboratory specimens to familiarize yourself with all types, sizes, and perspectives of the material.
- Start your review early, so as to avoid inconvenience and crowding in the laboratory in the days prior to the examination.
- If you believe the tag on a specimen has been altered during the examination, summon a supervisor immediately.

13
Confronting performance problems in examinations

This, the final chapter of the book, can be looked upon as a problem clinic. The preceding chapters have described how to prepare for your examinations and how to perform to the best of your potential once you have entered the examination room. However, examination candidates have occasionally incurred a variety of problems during the examination itself. This chapter addresses several of these problems, notably panic attacks, memory blocks, writer's cramp and general fatigue. The underlying assumption of this chapter is that you have prepared thoroughly for your examinations. Panic breeds upon uncertainty, so the more you know, the less likely you are to experience a panic attack. The best treatment for panic attacks and the other problems dealt with in this chapter is prevention.

Panic attacks

It seems that the experience of a panic attack hardly needs description. Most people have experienced at least a single panic attack, even if it was very brief and transient. Whether an attack has been experienced in an examination setting or not, the symptoms are very much the same. Typically, there is an accelerated heart beat, an increase in the breathing rate, sweating, and perhaps some shaking of the limbs. For examination candidates, the mental manifestations are the most important. Generally, the mind is awash with all sorts of catastrophic thoughts from: 'I'm going to fail!' to 'I don't know what I'm doing in this examination. I've got to get out!' Pressing on with an examination under these conditions is very difficult indeed.

As suggested above, the best treatment for panic attacks is prevention. If you have experienced panic attacks in previous examinations, it is best to work on the assumption that you could experience them again. Having faced this possibility, it is up to you to prepare yourself so thoroughly that there is little room for uncertainty to generate possible panic.

There are two major aspects to reducing the likelihood of future panic attacks. The first aspect concerns your study preparation—you should know the material as well as you possibly can so that your confidence is high on examination day. Most candidates who panic lack confidence in their preparation. Usually, they have left their review until late in the semester or year, and have discovered that they do not have time to learn all of the material sufficiently well to pass. Even if they can boost their courage and confidence on examination day, their courageous façade can be shattered very quickly by just one question which probes a weak study area. Therefore, students who are prone to panic attacks should be putting into practice the advice in the early chapters of this book—early and regular review. You should know the material so well that even if you strike a difficult question, you are able to think calmly about the answer instead of falling into a panic attack.

The second aspect of preparing for the possibility of a panic attack concerns mental control. The physical and mental manifestations of panic will not occur if you have tight and deliberate control over what your mind is doing. You might say: 'Of course I have control over my mind! Who else would be controlling it?' Most of us would like to believe we have that firm level of mental control which would preclude the possibility of panic, but the real situation is that very few examination candidates exercise careful control over what is happening in their minds. Certainly, they can focus their attention on the questions and search their minds for relevant information; but the crucial point is whether they can deal with the fleeting, anxiety-based thoughts related to their success or possible failure. Tight mental control is necessary in order to deal effectively with these tangential thoughts.

There are several ways in which an examination candidate can develop more effective control over their mental activity—by mental conditioning, by thought stopping and by positive suggestion. Each of these strategies will be discussed in turn.

Mental conditioning depends upon the establishment of a conditioned response in your mind. The situation is somewhat similar to a physical reflex, such as a knee jerk response. Instead of using a physical stimulus, a verbal one is better for the examination room. The object of the conditioning is to provide you with the ability to control your mind—to react firmly and positively to any anxiety-prone thoughts.

How is this mental conditioning established? There are two prerequisites. Firstly, you must start the conditioning process at least several months before the examination period. Conditioning takes time and PRACTICE—the second prerequisite. The actual conditioning technique has been described in Chapter Four (pps. 28-46). If you have practiced the relaxation training described in Chapter Four and if you are now able to elicit a strong relaxation response when you say the stimulus word, 'RELAX,' you are well on your way to controlling your wandering and panic-prone mind.

Now, what to do in the examination room when your mind strays off-course and becomes potentially panicky? At the very first hint of a possible panic attack (you will probably know the signs within yourself—lightheadedness, tingling in the fingers, dizziness, tightness in the stomach, to mention but a few possible signs) fix your eyes on a spot, or shut your eyes, and then say to yourself 'R-E—L-A-X.' See the letters R-E-L-A-X in your mind as you pronounce the word. Repeat it up to six times to break the feeling of panic. As your mind will be occupied with the word 'RELAX' in both the visual and auditory channels of your brain, there is little room for panic-prone thoughts. Repeat the process as many times as necessary.

A second strategy for preventing panic attacks is thought stopping. With this technique, you interrupt the panicky thoughts at their onset by visualizing a red and white STOP sign. While seeing the stop sign in your mind, say to yourself very firmly, 'STOP!' You can add a physical action as well, such as clenching a fist in time with saying 'STOP!.' Make the imaginary stop sign flash on and off six times while saying 'STOP!' At the end of the series, focus your attention on a non-threatening examination question and re-establish your confidence. You may have to repeat the sequence several times to prevent the panicky thoughts from getting a foothold in your mind. The stronger your control over what is happening in your mind, the less chance that panic will set in.

A third approach to dealing with imminent panic attacks is to slow down your breathing rate. Many examination candidates find that as they strike a difficult area of an examination, their breathing rate accelerates and becomes shallow. The end result of rapid and shallow breathing is that they become predisposed to anxiety and possibly panic. As soon as you recognize the first signs of anxiety and possible panic, think about your breathing. Take a long, slow and deep breath, allowing the air to flow out slowly and smoothly. Then maintain a regular breathing pattern, being very certain that you do not lapse into the rapid rate again.

If your breathing pattern has been rapid and shallow for some time, you might find that associated with feelings of anxiety, you are also feeling light-headed. It is possible that you have breathed out too much carbon dioxide, causing a temporary chemical imbalance. In order to re-establish the balance, cup your hands tightly and breathe into this contained space. Alternatively, breathe into a bag with your head lowered between your knees. These procedures will allow you to re-breathe some of the exhaled carbon dioxide and insure adequate blood circulation to your brain. If you feel awkward carrying out these procedures in the examination room, ask to leave the room and do them in the toilet. The important goal is to regain your metabolic and psychological equilibrium so that you can return to the examination and perform to the best of your ability.

A final technique to overcome panic in the examination room is to replace the negative thoughts, which almost always cause the panicky feelings, with a positive thought. How do you become a better and more frequent positive thinker? You are probably very familiar with the answer by now—PRACTICE. It might sound silly, but saying to yourself something like: 'I *CAN* pass that economics examination!,' many times a day can help to form a more positive attitude about the outcome of the examination. Repeating the positive statement builds a more positive attitude and also prevents you from entertaining negative statements. Plan a relevant positive statement and repeat it to yourself every time you pass through a doorway or carry out some other frequent activity. It really is surprising how such a simple technique can affect your thinking.

Memory blocks

Memory blocks would follow anxiety reactions in the list of common examination problems. Most of us can recall having at least one or more memory blocks in our past examination experiences. While they appear to be a common examination experience, they are certainly not welcome. Who wants to feel the pressure of the clock while trying to extract a familiar or even well-known fact or concept 'from the tip of the tongue'?

Just as with panic attacks, the best approach to memory blocks is prevention. The most common cause of memory blocks is inadequate preparation. Thus, in order to reduce the possibility of memory blocks, the best attack is a very thorough and regular review. Don't wait until the week before the examination to review your year's lecture notes. There is simply too much work to fit into the remaining time. Review daily and weekly throughout the year so the review chore at the end of the semester is realistic and achievable.

Should you experience a memory block in an examination, try the following. Rule number one is *don't panic*! Memory blocks seem to thrive in an up-tight environment. Take a calm, slow and deep breath and let the air out gently while you say 'RELAX' to yourself. When you have completed the slow breath, consider again the matter which you were trying to recall. If it still does not come to you, pass over the question, and come back to it later.

A second approach to retrieving a memory item utilizes mental associations. Think back to the lectures and your notes and try to recall facts and concepts which are associated with the blocked item. Jot down the concepts and see if you can draw some connecting lines between them. Where does the blocked item fit in the pattern? Are there any causal relationships or any other types of associations which you can use? What about information from other fields of your knowledge? For example, can you use your knowledge of history to help put a scientific achievement into perspective?

Should you draw a blank after working out the associations, try imagining yourself as the examiner who is writing the questions. See in your mind the question being written, and then the answer. Alternatively, imagine yourself as being the brightest student in your class and see your hand as being theirs. Let your hand start writing, even if you can write only one or two letters. See if those letters offer any clues or suggestions about the blocked item.

Another attack on the blocked item uses your ability to recall the page of your notes on which you recorded the item during the relevant lecture. If the item came from a book instead of a lecture, try to visualize the page in the textbook. Imagine what topics came just before and just after the blocked item and try to fill in the gap.

A final approach to retreiving a blocked item uses the other questions in the examination as possible levers. In objective examinations, where you are likely to have a large number of questions, it is possible that a subsequent question might give you a clue. Keep in mind the question where you incurred the block. If you strike a related or relevant question, see if any of the terms spark a helpful association.

As mentioned above, memory blocks are best treated preventively. It is worthwhile to note that if, as you are progressing through your examination, you remember a few helpful facts which you know are relevant to another question in the examination, take a few seconds and jot them down in the margin of the test booklet. The few seconds are well spent; you would be very annoyed if you pressed on and then were not able to recall the items which were readily retrieveable and a few minutes previously. While your memory is generally quite reliable, it is best not to take the risk of a block during the actual examination.

Writer's cramp

Sitting in an examination for several hours and writing virtually non-stop is a tiring experience for most people. The concentration, the time pressure and the concern for legibility of the script go together to create the possibility of writer's cramp. The problem, as suggested above, has two components, muscular tension and psychological stress.

At the risk of being unduly repetitive, the best approach to the problem of writer's cramp is prevention. Rather than preventing the problem totally, the preventive approach is more a process of conditioning or training. Just as an athlete trains assiduously to perfect his or her performance, the examination candidate who has had trouble with hand cramps during examinations must also train so that the problem is minimized or eliminated altogether.

The training program should include a conditioning regimen for the hand and arm muscles as well as psychological conditioning. The muscle training program is what you have probably already anticipated—practice sessions which simulate the actual examination conditions. Start with practice sessions lasting perhaps one hour.

In that hour, write continuously for three fifteen-minute periods with a five minute break between each writing period. In order to use the time productively, you might practice writing out summaries of the work on which you will be examined later. When you have been able to write for three fifteen-minute periods with *legible* handwriting (a classmate should read the summaries or sample answers which you have written), increase the time periods by five or ten minutes. Continue the program until you are able to write for periods which are as long as you will have for the questions on your examination. During the examination, take frequent short breaks and allow your hand to dangle limply at your side. You might find mild shaking of the hand or alternate contracting and relaxing your hand to be helpful. The important thing is to allow for the breaks so that the hand does not build up tension to the cramping level.

The psychological pressure can be alleviated by eliminating as many of the examination uncertainties as possible. Refer to Chapter Six (pp 53-63) for a detailed discussion about the sources of uncertainty which should be clarified prior to the examination. In addition to knowing what to expect in the examination, you will want to walk into the examination room with the highest possible level of preparation. Finally, you will want to be able to release psychological stress and strain by calling up a relaxation response (see Chapter Four, pp 28-46). By pairing the muscle conditioning with a positive psychological preparation, you will be able to approach your examinations with a more relaxed and assured attitude.

Physical fatigue

The last examination problem to be dealt with in this chapter is general physical fatigue. Many examination candidates are likely to underrate this problem, primarily because of the sedentary nature of the examination process. However, if the candidate has been working very hard and extending the study hours into sleep time in the weeks preceding the examinations, fatigue is likely to be a problem.

Just as a conditioning program was recommended for the problem of a writer's cramp, or fatigue of the hand muscles, a similar program is recommended for generalized fatigue. It is very important that the sleep hours are not reduced drastically over the long term. Chronic tiredness from inadequate sleep will affect your examination performance, although the loss of a few hours on the night before your examination is not likely to be a significant deterrant. In addition to getting adequate and regular sleep, be careful about your diet. Avoid stimulants, either in the form of caffeinated drinks or as non-prescribed medications. Your metabolism is probably going to be stimulated enough by the examination without any additional help from foods or drugs. Try to get some daily exercise to keep your body muscles in tone and to give yourself the opportunity to burn off some of the pre-examination emotional tensions.

During the examination take occasional breaks by stretching your arms, your neck and back, and then your legs. If you feel tense and tight and this feeling is impeding your examination performance, ask a supervisor if you can be excused to go to the toilet. Take the opportunity to splash some water over your face and to do some further stretching exercises while in the toilet. The few minutes you are away from the examination can give you a fresh start on your return.

SUMMARY

The problems of panic attacks, memory blocks, writer's cramp and general physical fatigue are all best dealt with by prevention—start early, prepare and practice. Additional guidelines are summarized below:

Panic attacks

- Practice mental control by excluding panic-prone thoughts.
- Develop a strong relaxation response which can be applied in the examination room.
- Keep your breathing rate slow and regular.
- Replace negative thoughts with positive ones.

Memory blocks

- Jot down concepts associated with the blocked item and look for connecting links.
- Imagine yourself as the lecturer writing the question and noting the correct response. See the question from alternate points of view.
- Use other examination questions as springboards or levers to prompt your thinking towards the blocked item.

Writer's cramp

- Train your hand muscles to sustain increasing periods of writing under simulated examination conditions.
- Occasionally allow your hand to dangle limply at your side to relieve the stress and tension.

Physical fatigue

- Be certain not to cut drastically your sleep hours over the long term. You will need to be alert during the examination period.
- Stretch your limbs at frequent intervals during the examination to relieve tension.
- Splash cold water over your face in the toilet if you feel very tired and mentally dull.

Appendix

External secondary education examinations

- Start preparing for your examinations early by collecting information about previous examinations. Having read previous papers and talked to some of last year's candidates, you will recognize examinable topics when they arise during the present year.
- Review systematically and routinely each week by going over the week's notes. Set aside a regular time for the review so that it becomes part of your weekly routine. Systematic weekly review is the best way to deal with examination nerves because you will *know* that you know the material if you have been reviewing regularly throughout the year.

- If personal discipline is in short supply, arrange to meet a conscientious classmate for these regular review sessions. Be sure to keep your minds on the appointed task.

- For those students who are starting their review at a later point in the year, organize a timetable which allows for several reviews of your notes and other materials. Focus upon the major topics of your first review. Having gone through your notes thoroughly, go through them again, this time picking up the sub-topics and supporting details. If time allows, try to read, recite and write the topics with note headings under each. Being able to write these notes is the acid test of whether you know the material.

- If examination nerves have been a problem for you in the past, consult your school counselor or a professional psychologist early in the year so that adequate time is available to work upon the problem. Read Chapter Four in this book to learn how to relax yourself before your examinations begin.

- Be certain that in the weeks preceding your examinations that you get sufficient rest. You will want to be alert and clear-thinking during your examination period.

- Your preparation for your examinations should reflect the nature of each subject. You should focus upon problem-solving in mathematics and essay writing in humanities subjects. Review your laboratory exercises in science subjects and be certain that you are knowledgeable about graph interpretation in the social sciences.

- Use the subject syllabus as a general guide for your review. It is fair to assume that the examinations will reflect the importance of the topics listed in the syllabus.

- Avoid preparing set answers and then writing them out in parrot fashion during the examination. The examiners will quickly recognize essays which do not address the specific issues raised in the questions. Remember, you will want to demonstrate your abilities to interpret the questions, organize your thoughts and write clear, concise and logically argued essays.

- If you are weak in essay writing, start early in the year to improve your skills. Ask your teachers if they would mind reading several mini-essays and giving you some suggestions for improvement. Writing, writing, and more writing is the only sure way to improve your essay writing ability.

- Talk to your teachers and classmates about the differences which you can expect in the examinations for which you will be sitting. You will want to know if it is permissible to use headings in your science subject essays and whether you can use a calculator for problem solving. If calculators are permitted, ask whether it is necessary to show on paper the steps through which the final answer was derived.

- Get organized early and be certain that your review covers the syllabus adequately. Be aware of your personal examination strengths and weaknesses, and cater for these differences in your review program. Strengthening your skills and being determined, disciplined and organized in your review will help to produce a successful outcome.

The medical viva examination

The medical viva examination is a form of assessment used to evaluate the diagnostic and communication skills of medical students and medical graduates who are candidates for specialty memberships or fellowships. The examination usually requires the candidate to examine several patients, one at a time, and then answer questions at the bedside. The following notes have been collected from individuals who have passed the viva examination in the medical course at the University of New South Wales.

- Be certain to have many practice runs with hospital teaching staff before the examination date.
- Practice thinking quickly and clearly with classmates by testing each other in simulated viva situations.
- Do not assume the absence of positive feedback (or any feedback) from examiners means you are doing poorly. Many examiners approach the examination with practiced 'stone' or 'poker' faces.
- Candidates who keep up a stream of constructive chatter maintain control of the examination. Provide relevant information to the examiners (especially in your strong knowledge areas) and do not wait to be asked for further details.
- Do not fabricate tests and procedures if you can't justify their use.
- If you can't respond to a question, say that you don't know and ask if you can go on to another area of questioning.
- If embarrassment is a problem for you, practice becoming

embarrassed with classmates who are taking the examiner's role. Learn how to deal with your embarrassment by confronting the problem—don't avoid the problem by pretending it does not exist.

- Establish set routines for examining the chest, abdomen, etc. Be positive and thorough with the basics, but do not waste the examiner's time by being excessively pedantic.
- Organize your facts and information in a systems approach. Each fact brings to mind related facts and issues.
- During ward rounds, do not habitually stand in the back row of the group, hoping to avoid being called upon. Learn by trying and by sometimes making mistakes. Be visible, be willing to have a go, and be prepared to think under pressure. It has often been said that the only people who are not making mistakes are those who are either stagnant or dead.
- Seek help early from clinical staff if you feel that you are at risk of failing.
- Try to anticipate the types of cases you are likely to be given and prepare with a group of classmates.
- If a question is asked which you believe to be ambiguous, ask for clarification or a re-phrasing of the question.
- Do not rush into your answers—take time to think the question through and then present a well-organized response.
- If a hasty and incorrect answer has been given, say so straight away, and ask if you can offer a more considered response.
- When you are uncertain about a specific question, start with a general, but relevant point and work towards a more specific answer. While you are giving yourself time to think, be cautious about appearing to waste the examiner's time.
- Do not be alarmed if the examiner appears to be asking a question which is too easy. Go ahead and give the obvious answer.
- Approach the viva examination with the expectation that you will pass. Be positive! Remind yourself about your previous positive performances and accomplishments in academic and non-academic areas.
- Start your preparation for your viva examination early. Develop your skills in thinking decisively and logically. Be certain that you know the basics and that you can call up in your mind the necessary lists, characteristics, tests, etc. for the common medical complaints.

- Do not expect to be able to answer every single question in the examination. It is often the case that particularly difficult questions are used in the examination to differentiate the very superior from the superior candidates.
- Even though there is a 'performance' element in the viva examination, the basic issues which the examiners want to know are whether you know your material well and whether you can use your knowledge in the applied setting. Therefore, the single most important aspect should be knowing your material. Take time each week to review your work so that you can approach the viva with a confident feeling.

Civil service entrance examinations

Civil service authorities generally use various types of examinations to screen applicants for specific types of jobs. The examinations are generally held several times a year. Based upon the results, a short list will be formed and candidates successful in the examination will be called in for interviews prior to the final selection.

- Telephone the department which administers the civil service entrance examinations to obtain the relevant details—the date, time and place of the next examination, and any necessary materials which you should bring to the examination.
- Ask about the type(s) of tests which you will be asked to take. You may wish to inquire about the topical areas upon which they will focus. For example, you may want to know whether your mathematical abilities will be assessed or whether there will be a test of your general information. Inquire as well about suggested preparation strategies for the tests.
- Civil service entrance examinations often include aptitude tests to assess the candidate's potential for using skills associated with the relevant job. Tests of verbal comprehension, expression, mathematics, and clerical speed and accuracy are typically given in the aptitude test battery.
- Verbal comprehension tests are designed to measure your ability to read and understand various types of written material. The written passages may be letters, reports or other types of business documents. Practice by reading an assortment of annual reports and business magazines to prepare

your mind for the comprehension test. Ask a friend or relative to quiz you on the documents after you have read them.

- The mathematics test will probably be restricted to basic mathematical functions. If you feel a bit shaky about your mathematics ability, obtain a basic mathematics textbook from your local library or school and practice solving some sample problems. Ask a local teacher to help you if you strike any difficulties.

- Tests of clerical speed and accuracy measure the candidate's ability to check columns of figures or textual material for errors. As is obvious from the title of these tests, both speed and accuracy are very important. You will need to be mentally alert and perceptive. Be certain that you enter the examination room in a well-rested state.

- For certain types of technical and trade positions, you may be asked to take an achievement test. These tests measure your knowledge and skills in the relevant area. They may dwell upon concepts and skills which form part of a relevant technical school curriculum, so reviewing your notes from previous technical courses should be helpful.

- Tests of technical and vocational skills are given to applicants for specific jobs, such as stenographers and typists. You should prepare for these tests by practicing the relevant skills. If your skills are a bit rusty, give yourself adequate preparation time before you schedule yourself for the examination.

- Candidates who are invited for an interview should bear in mind that government departments are generally conservative in nature. Therefore, think about your appearance and clothes. Attending the interview in attire which is considered to be radical or anti-establishment is not likely to enhance your chances of being employed. Male applicants should consider whether wearing a tie and jacket is appropriate and female applicants may want to think about the suitability of their various outfits. If in doubt, ask friends who work in the civil service for their advice.

- Read through the list of questions commonly asked during employment interviews (Appendix p 141) and prepare answers for those questions which you think are relevant to your interview.

- Some civil service appointments are specifically for certain regional offices. Consider before the interview how far you are willing to travel to work each day.

- Write down on a card the questions which you want to ask in the interview. Most interviewers will ask if you have any questions and you can show initiative by having several questions prepared. Of course, don't go over areas which have already been discussed in the interview.
- Should there be a delay of more than a few weeks in hearing about the results of your interview, do not hesitate to telephone the department and ask about the progress of your application.
- Should your initial application be unsuccessful, consider the strengths and weaknesses of your first attempt and then have another go. It is important to look upon each attempt as a learning experience, even if there are some negative outcomes. Practice does help, especially for individuals willing to learn from their experiences.

Auditions in the performing arts

- Contact the theater, agency, school or institution for whom you intend to audition to obtain as early as possible the relevant details (date, time and place of the auditions and the work(s) to be prepared).
- Try to establish who will be auditioning you. What is their background? What are their likes and dislikes? Any information about the judges will help you in your preparation.
- If time permits, talk to friends and colleagues who are established in the relevant field and ask for their advice on your work and audition material.
- Visit the place where your audition is to be held so that you are familiar with the surroundings and any problems posed by the space (for example, a small stage, background noise, poor lighting). Try to accommodate these limitations when rehearsing for your audition.
- Prepare and practice your audition work *very* thoroughly. The more prepared you are, the more relaxed and confident you are likely to be.
- Prior to the audition day, perform your work in front of several knowledgeable friends and experienced colleagues. Ask for detailed and constructive criticism on your performance.
- Make any adjustments to your performance which you think are justified on the basis of the feedback from your friends and colleagues.

- Following your intensive and thorough preparation period, get a good night's rest before the day of the audition. See the relevant chapters in this book on fear control and positive thinking to help overcome excessive nervousness.
- Arrive sufficiently early before your appointed time so that you have plenty of warmup time. Doing some vigourous exercises can help loosen your body and release nervous tension.
- If, while waiting for your turn, you are watching the performances of those ahead of you, be sure that you are not making unjust comparisons between their performances and your ability. If your mind deviates from positive thinking, hold it in line by saying something like: 'I know my work and I can perform it well!' over and over to yourself.
- Should the jitters and shakes begin to affect you, close your eyes, take a slow and deep breath and then let the air out gently while saying 'RELAX' to yourself.
- When you are called, pause for a few seconds before getting up. Compose yourself mentally and physically. Another slow, deep breath will be helpful.
- In some auditions, you are likely to be stopped midway through your performance. The comments offered during the interruption might be tactful, but they could also be abrasive. Accept the remarks objectively and do not take any criticism personally.
- If your are unsuccessful in your audition, contact the auditioning authority or agency for an interview a few days later. Ask for feedback on how you can improve your performance, or your auditioning skills.

Time-saving for part-time students

While most professionals who are preparing for certification or fellowship examinations will quickly agree that each discipline will have its own examination specifications and requirements, most candidates will be faced with the common problem and grueling ordeal of having to study part-time, work full-time and fulfill their personal and domestic responsibilities in the remaining time. The critical challenge for candidates preparing for their professional certification examinations is finding sufficient time to study. This checklist addresses the issue of saving time or using effectively previously wasted time. The checklist specifies seven time wasting situations and then presents possible strategies for using your time more effectively in these situations.

Telephone calls

Calls to others:

- Plan for a telephone call period daily and do them in bulk.
- Plan each call. What are your objectives? How long should the call take?
- Be prepared to say, 'I've got to go now,' to the other party to terminate the call.
- Use the telephone instead of writing a letter. You can get the response immediately.

Calls from others:

- Have all calls screened, if possible.
- If you do not want to be disturbed, take the receiver off the hook.
- Do not avoid telling the caller that you are busy and that you will call back when free (establish a call-back time, if possible).
- For frequent callers, tell them when you would prefer to have them call you rather than be interrupted at inopportune times.

Television

- Read the program guide and decide which shows warrant watching.
- Realize that turning the TV on requires little energy, but turning it off can be a challenge.
- Set an egg timer or alarm to go off at the end of programs to be viewed.
- If you want to watch only the news, stay standing. Do not sit down.
- The definitive solution for the poor self-disciplinarians—sell the set or give it away.

Meetings

- If you are very busy, convey your apology for not attending.
- Suggest to the group prior to the meeting that an agenda be issued and it be followed.

- If your time is being wasted in the meeting, excuse yourself and leave.
- Suggest that discussions be time-limited in the meeting.
- Suggest that regular meetings be cancelled if there is no important business to be discussed.
- Use circulars and memoranda rather than calling a large meeting simply to read out a list of non-urgent matters.

Waiting

- Carry a book with you so you can read during waiting periods.
- Plan ahead and anticipate waits. Use the time before a meeting, appointment or class to prime your mind or review notes.
- If you expect that you will be kept waiting, ring ahead to see if the person is running late. Establish a revised appointment time.
- If you are often kept waiting by a person whom you see regularly, discuss the matter tactfully.

Travel

- Time in your car or on public transport can be used productively. Organize your day, prepare mentally for meetings, study note cards or close your eyes and use the time to relax.
- In your car, make notes on a mini-recorder or on paper at red lights or in traffic jams.
- On crowded buses or trains, use small review cards held together with string or a metal ring and review formulae, factual material and other study notes. Use the same study notes for quick review spurts while waiting in bank lines, cafeteria lines and other 'waiting' places.
- On planes, take correspondence which must be answered, notes to be reviewed for the next appointment, or professional background reading which relates to your certification studies.
- Always be prepared for long delays (such as transport delays, 'no show' appointments) and have enough study material with you so that you can use the time effectively.

Drop-in visitors

- Keep your office door closed if you do not want to be disturbed.

- Screen visitors via your secretary, or by placing a tactfully worded note on your door.
- Go to others before they come to you. It is far easier to terminate a brief meeting if you are in control of the time. Simply say: 'I've got to dash.'
- If a garrulous colleague does come to your office and you are pressed for time, stand in the doorway and discuss the matter there.
- If the colleague gets into your office, do not sit down and do not offer the person a seat. Standing conferences are much shorter than sitting ones.

Inability to say, "NO!"

- Anticipate meetings and events where pressure will be placed on you to take on responsibilities which you do not want to accept.
- Practice saying 'NO!' to the bathroom mirror. Exaggerate the word, say it emphatically. With practice, it's much easier to say 'NO!' in public.
- Saying 'NO!' assertively (a positive and constructive communication) can be a complex and delicate task. Read a self-help book on becoming more assertive so that you can protect your time and energy for your important goals.

References

Alan MacKenzie. *The Time Trap*. N.Y.: McGraw-Hill, 1975.
Alan Lakein. *How to get control of your time and your life*. N.Y.: Futura Books, 1979.

The Job Interview (a form of verbal examination)

- On receiving an appointment for a job interview, telephone the prospective employer to accept the appointment and to confirm the date, time and place of the interview.
- During the telephone call, ascertain if possible, who the interviewer(s) will be.
- Following the telephone call, start collecting information about the company, the relevant department and the members of the interviewing committee if possible. Obtain, if relevant, last year's annual report and any other documents pertinent to

the firm or department so you can learn about their present activities.

- If you have questions about the job or if you feel you would like to meet the person under whom you will be working, try to arrange a personal interview prior to the date of the scheduled interview. You will probably be more relaxed in a one-to-one situation and hence will be able to create a better impression. Requesting such an interview can also show enthusiasm and keenness.

- Write down questions which you think might be asked during the shortlist interview. Arrange for a friend to ask these questions under simulated interview conditions and practice your responses. It is important to be able to respond naturally and fluently and not in parrot fashion. See the following checklist for possible interview questions.

- Check with friends and job colleagues to see what is the most appropriate type of clothing to wear to the interview. Hair style can also be a concern. Remember, how you present yourself physically is the first communication of the interview. Give careful thought to your appearance.

- Prepare a list of questions to carry into the interview for the inevitable question: 'Do you have any questions which you would like to ask us?' Consulting your list at this point can show preparedness and thoroughness. If all the pertinent issues have been dealt with, say: 'No, we seem to have covered all of the important points.' Think twice about raising issues about holidays, special leave and sickness benefits which might be misinterpreted by the committee. There is ample time to get these details sorted out after you are offered the job.

- Practice pause responses so that you are not shaken by totally unanticipated questions. Time is on your side and taking a few seconds to think can create an impression of confidence—confidence to remain in control of yourself and the time.

- Practice regaining control over anxiety feelings by taking a slow, deep breath during simulated interviews.

- Practice maintaining appropriate eye contact with all members of the (simulated) interview committee.

- On the day of the interview, be certain to allow time for mishaps and misadventure (flat tire, road detours, etc.) so that you are not late.

- Have pen and paper with you for any notes which you might want to take.

- Take along some interesting and absorbing reading material so that you do not sit and worry for long periods prior to your interview.
- Before you are called into the interview room, check to see that your hair and clothes are as you want them.
- When called, enter the interview room in a positive and confident fashion.
- During the interview, do not fall prey to the 'slippery seat syndrome.' That is, do not progressively allow your body to slide into a more prone position, giving an ultra 'laid back' impression. Your body language (eye contact, gestures, posture, facial expressions, etc.) is continually communicating important information to your interviewers.
- After the interview, think back over the strong and weak points so that you can improve your 'performance skills' if you are not selected for the position.

Possible questions in an employment interview

- Why do you want to work for this organization?
- How has your background prepared you for the position for which you are applying?
- What other employment possibilities are you considering at the moment?
- Do you have any special skills and abilities which we should know about?
- How has your academic background prepared you for this particular job?
- (If appropriate) Why did you leave your previous job?
- What charactistics make you a desirable candidate for this job?
- Looking ahead five years, what position do you think you will be filling?
- Should a transfer to a different place be necessary, how do you feel about traveling further each day or perhaps even moving interstate?
- What do you most value in a job?
- Overtime and some weekend work might be necessary. How do you think these arrangements will fit into your personal life?
- What hobbies and interests do you pursue in your free time?
- What personal characteristics are likely to present the greatest

difficulty for you, should you be appointed to the position?
- What personal qualities have limited or enhanced your work performance in your previous positions?
- If you were to specify your own salary for this job, how much would you pay yourself?
- If you were a member of this interviewing committee, how would you see yourself as an applicant for the position?
- We've been asking all of the questions so far. Do you have any questions which you would like to ask us?

Motor vehicle drivers' test

- Consult your state authorities for information about the driving laws and the driving test.
- Obtain a copy of the driving laws upon which your verbal or written test will be based.
- Study the laws and rules thoroughly.
- Arrange for a driving instructor to teach you the skills of driving. If a family member or friend offers their talent and time, consider their competency, and the insurance cover on their vehicle.
- Generally speaking, it will be cheaper to practice with a friend, but you might be learning their bad habits.
- Practice the driving skills which you will be asked to perform in your test.
- Determine from the state authority whether being tested in an automatic versus a manual car will place a restriction upon your driver's licence.
- Find an easy and difficult location to practice each driving skill. For example, a three point turn is easier on a flat wide street versus a hilly narrow street. Practice your skill in reverse parking on flat then hilly streets.
- Practice sessions should initially be carried out in streets with little or no traffic.
- Reward yourself for successfully completing each new skill.
- If you fail in performing a particular driving skill, ask you driving teacher for a step by step analysis so you can understand what you did well and not so well.
- Between practice sessions, think through the integral steps of, for example, a three-point-turn. Pretend you are in the driver's seat and go through the steps one by one in your lounge room.

At your next practice session in the car, your mind, hands and feet will have the order of events well-synchronized.

- Try to preserve and practice your sense of humor. A frayed temper is counter-productive when trying to learn how to drive.
- If you feel yourself getting tense and nervous, take a slow, deep breath and let the air out gently. Say 'RELAX' to yourself as you exhale.
- On the day of your driving test, keep your mind fruitfully occupied and busy so you don't have time to worry about the test.
- Avoid drinking copious amounts of tea and coffee prior to your test. Too much caffeine (more than two or three cups) can make you feel jittery and will increase the filling rate of your bladder.
- If a worry or negative thought starts, say forcefully to yourself 'STOP!' Replace the negative thought with a positive one, such as 'I CAN PASS!'
- If you are a bit nervous when you meet your examiner, tell the person you are nervous. This will not be a new situation to the examiner and talking and perhaps even laughing a bit about the situation will help you feel more comfortable.
- If you wish to smoke during your test, ask the examiner for permission. Smoking in the car with a non-smoker will not increase your chances of passing.
- If you fail to perform successfully one of the skills during the test, ask the examiner what you did incorrectly. You might be able to try that section of the test again, perhaps in a different location.
- In the event of a total freeze-up of your mind and body, ask the examiner if you can get out of the car for a breath of fresh air and a stretch. Loosening up your body by stretching, shaking your hands, arms, legs and feet will help to release some of the built-up tension. Take a slow, deep breath and then get back into the car to resume the test.
- During the test, and just prior to one of your difficult maneuvers, pause for a few moments before beginning the maneuver and run through the steps mentally.
- If, during stressful conditions, you tend to become dry in the mouth, take along some lozenges.
- If the result of your examination is a failure, do not let the

outcome be a source of depression or confidence erosion. Ask yourself immediately what new aspects you learned from the examination, and plan how these new insights will help you in your next attempt.

- If anxiety and body coordination are major problems for you and they have hindered you in passing your driving test(s), consider consulting a professional psychologist. A listing of professionally qualified psychologists will be found in the Yellow Pages telephone directory.